# daredevil DREAMER

# TIM O'CONNOR

First published in 2019 by Denim Publications

ISBN: 978-0-578-60872-3



*Daredevil Dreamer* is a work of non-fiction.
Some names and identifying details have been changed.



Tim O'Connor asserts the moral right to be identified as the author of this work.

Cover photography:
*Kenn Santos*

# TABLE OF CONTENTS

*For Billie-Rose,*
*who inspired me to write what I know,*
*for Henson & Phoenix,*
*who I strive to make proud every day,*
*for all at Harvest Rain*
*who bravely stand by my side,*
*and for all the Dreamers*
*who dare to dream big dreams.*

*Onwards!*

# AUTHOR'S NOTE

Before we begin, I must make a confession.

I have a terrible memory.

Most days by lunch time I'm pretty hazy on the details of what I had for breakfast let alone the details of things that happened to me twenty or thirty years ago, so writing this book really stretched the bounds of my memory bank!  As such, it's important to note that the events recounted in this book are based on my best recollections. This is not a detailed memoir, a historical document, or a documentary. These are my stories as I remember them, lovingly recalled here for the purposes of illustrating how life taught me to dream big and live brave.  The details may have grown fuzzy over the years, but the lessons remain crystal clear, and those lessons - and the essence of the events that inspired them - is what you will find contained herein.

Enjoy!

# OVERTURE
# THE BOARD OF DREAMERS

Oprah stared at me from across the room.

Her face didn't give away much – her brow furrowed as her mouth cracked a gentle smile.

I think she was approving.

Steven Spielberg smirked at me from across the way, too. It was that cheeky, mischievous beam that had spurred me on to many a big adventure in the past, and there he was, once again egging me on with his knowing grin.

I looked over to Jim Henson - the man behind the Muppets who had singlehandedly revolutionised puppetry and television and children's entertainment - and tried to gauge his face for any sign of endorsement. His bushy beard almost obscured his mouth entirely, so it was hard to tell if he was smiling, but his gentle eyes conveyed warmth and understanding that always brought me solace.

I think he approved.

I never did anything without running it past those three first.

They were my Board of Dreamers, my go-to guides for just about every major decision I had ever made, not just in my job as the head of the largest youth arts organization in the world, but in my personal life too.

When I had to resolve a dispute between staff members, I turned to Oprah for guidance.

When I had a bold idea to pitch or a big vision for something new I wanted to do with the company, I looked to Steven for advice.

When I felt lost, or burnt out, or out of options, or backed into a corner, or helpless or alone, I went to Jim for comfort.

And they always came through for me, one way or another.

Of course, I'd never met any of them in actual real life.

Oprah and Steven lived half a world away from my home in Australia, and Jim had died when I was just a kid, but their pictures hung in a row on the wall of my office at Harvest Rain, right across from my desk, and they looked down at me each day, like guardian angels watching over me as I worked. I had put their photos there intentionally, as a daily reminder of the kind of person I wanted to be.

I wanted to be passionate and inspiring, like Oprah.

I wanted to be playful and imaginative, like Steven.

I wanted to be kind and courageous, like Jim.

They were the dreamers of big dreams, and I wanted to be a

dreamer just like them, and so each day as I looked up from my desk at their faces, I would think to myself "What would Oprah do?", or "What would Steven say?" or "What would Jim think?" And if I sat quietly and waited for their answer, usually it would come. I had devoured every book that was ever written about their lives and read every word they had ever put to paper, so when I looked to them for guidance I only ever needed to recall their words or their stories to find an answer to whatever challenge I was facing. They had never let me down, my Board of Dreamers, and on this day, I needed them more than ever.

Harvest Rain had been producing traditional musicals in traditional theatres for almost three decades, but I had come up with this crazy idea to present our work in an entirely new format. I wanted to stage a well-known musical in large Entertainment Centre arenas featuring hundreds of young performers on stage, kind of like if a musical and an Olympics opening ceremony had a love child. As far as concepts go, it was pretty out there, but I knew if we could pull it off, it would be record-breaking - a world first - a whole new genre of theatre and a life-changing opportunity for a myriad of young performers to be part of such a spectacle.

It would also cost millions of dollars to produce.

We didn't have millions of dollars.

We didn't have any dollars.

With no financial backing, I was gambling that over ten thousand people would come and see this new arena show, and those ticket sales would pay for the production, and then on we would go from there. It was a huge risk, and as I sat in my office staring up at Oprah, Steven and Jim, I examined their faces for any sign that I should dare to take the punt. My Board of Dreamers had made their dreams all come true – would the same thing happen for me, I wondered. As I scanned their faces for approval, I realised that there was really only one person I could turn to for permission to dare, and his face lived in the mirror, not in a photo on my wall.

Our Business Manager appeared at my door, looking a little sheepish as he clutched his note pad and pen. I'd told the Harvest Rain staff about my big vision for shows in the arena earlier that day, and from the look on his face, it was clear he had been feverishly breathing into a paper bag in his office ever since the meeting had adjourned.

"How are we going to pull this off?" he questioned as he sat down gingerly on my couch, directly beneath Oprah, Steven and Jim.

"I'm still figuring that out," I replied. "But I feel pretty good about it. I think we can pull this off."

"But it's so much money," he said, looking like he might like to regurgitate his lunch into my waste-paper basket. "What if it doesn't work?"

"We'll make it work," I said, defiantly, looking up to my Dreamers for back up. They just smiled. "I'm not afraid of having a big vision. I'm a dreamer, after all."

"No, you're a daredevil," he said.

"Well, maybe I'm a little bit of both."

Oprah, Steven and Jim smiled down at me.

After years of staring up at them for wisdom, in that instant, I finally worked out exactly what it was about them that I should actually be trying to emulate.

My Board of Dreamers did more than just dream their dreams. They didn't just come up with a good idea and then wait around for it to magically materialise in their reality.

They were not passive.

They were not lucky.

They were tenacious in the pursuit of their dreams.

They were relentless.

Unwavering.

Determined.

Unstoppable.

They saw a vision in their mind, and they went after it - despite the risk and despite the cost – they doggedly followed their dream until it came to fruition. In wanting to be like them, I had misunderstood something fundamental about each of them.

They were not just dreamers.

They were daredevils too.

In the days, months and years since that moment of realisation, I've learnt a thing or two about dreaming big and living brave (and I've staged sold-out arena productions of all sorts of musicals featuring hundreds of performers seen by tens of thousands of people, but more about that later!). I have come to discover that dreaming big is only one part of the equation; for those dreams to have a life you must also be prepared to live brave. The dream requires the dare. It's not enough to just dream it; for your dreams to come true, you have to also be brave enough to pursue them.

I've made a career out of doing that.

I've made a whole life out of it.

It's what I do.

It's who I am.

I have fought my dreams into reality.

I have forged on in the face of fear.

When I have fallen, I have refused to stay down.

I have run further than I thought I could run and climbed higher than I thought I could climb, all in an effort to chase my vision out into the light.

I am a Daredevil Dreamer.

Dreaming big and living bravely is what I do.

Written on the pages of this book are ten lessons I have learnt about ushering your dreams into reality; ten lessons that life has taught me about courageously pursuing the life you desire. It is everything I know about opening your mind to what is possible and then moving forward boldly until your reality reflects your dreams.

If you want to dream big dreams, but don't feel brave…

If you have a vision to pursue, but don't know how…

If you dare to own your destiny…

Then read on, friends.

Come daredevil dreaming with me.

## CHAPTER ONE
# HUNGRY DREAMS

When I was a kid, if daydreaming had been a sport, then I could have made it to the Olympics.

Dreaming was what I did best.

It was all I was really good at.

I wasn't sporty like most other kids. Running and sweating never rated highly on my list of exciting things to do, and I never understood why anyone would kick a ball around in the hot sun when you had the option of building a cubby house, or playing pretend, or accidentally lighting your trampoline on fire, or cutting the arms off all of your toys. I'm not saying I did any of those things....

Well, okay, I may have done some of them....

Oh, alright, alright. I did all of them.

I was curious and free-spirited, caught up in daydreams, and fascinated by making up my own games and adventures, finding my own fun and making my own way.

That's how the trampoline caught on fire, because I was trying to make a backyard campfire, and the trampoline just got in the way.

And that's why I cut the arms off all my toys because, like most children, I grew up watching *Sesame Street* and wanted a puppet of my own, so I took to my toys with the kitchen scissors, relieved them of all their stuffing and creating a bedroom full of misshapen muppets in the process. My Mother had an absolute fit about it (by some miracle, she never found out about the trampoline so please don't tell her). She thought I was defacing my toys, but the way I saw it, I was enhancing them. As I went to sleep at night, I would lie in bed dreaming up ideas for new puppets I could make from my toys, and when I woke at the crack of dawn the next morning, I simply had to enact the plan I had dreamed the night before. It wasn't enough for me to just think about those puppets and wish that I had one of my own – what I saw in my head simply had to be realized.

I would stage elaborate shows in my living room with my make-shift puppets, and any family member who wandered by would be forced to watch. They were full-blown one-man productions, usually centering around a fairytale or storybook or a movie I'd seen. Once I even re-enacted *The Wizard of Oz*, by rolling out a ream of computer paper to serve as the yellow brick road, sticking our Christmas tree at the end of it as a makeshift Emerald City. I then donned a pair of Mum's high heels for ruby slippers and skipped up and down the computer paper all afternoon pretending I was Judy Garland. Some days I'd turn our whole rumpus room into a movie studio or puppet theatre or cabaret venue, depending on what my imagination was conjuring up that day. Once, I dragged half the garden into my bedroom because I'd been reading C.S Lewis's famous book *The Lion, The Witch and the Wardrobe* and I wanted to create the forests of Narnia in our house. I had giant palm leaves hanging from the ceiling fan and bark and leaves everywhere. My Mother put her foot down when I emptied all the grass clippings from the lawn mower out onto my bedspread. I was trying to make an authentic Narnian wonderland, but Mum said I was just making a mess. Looking back, she was right, but in my mind, I was just feeding my dreams.

That's the thing about dreams.

They get hungry.

They want to be fed.

They start out as a curiosity when something catches your attention or sparks your imagination. It's like a little light goes on inside of you, a little flickering candle, the germ of an idea. Every time you think about it, the light grows a little brighter and a little brighter, with every thought, your dream gets fed, and it grows bigger and bigger. The light shines brighter and brighter, and before you know it the dream is big enough to demand your attention, to guide your every thought, to be the filter through which you look towards your future.

You feed it, it continues to grow and grow until you have no choice but to birth those dreams into reality.

That is the way of our dreams.

On my eleventh birthday, my Mother surprised me by taking me to see a live stage production of *The Wizard of Oz* at the Queensland Performing Arts Centre in Brisbane, the city where I lived in the northern part of Australia. It was my first real trip to the theatre ever. I was mesmerised by the lavish production and the eye-popping sets and costumes - it trumped my living room presentations, that was for sure! I was completely transfixed as I watched my favourite movie unfold before my eyes, brought to life by real singers and real dancers on a real theatre stage!

Oh, the stage!

It called to me and beckoned me throughout the whole performance. I don't know what was so alluring about it, but I just wanted to be up there on that stage, singing and dancing and being part of the theatre magic.

A light flickered on inside me, and from that day onwards as I went to sleep each night, my dreams of defacing toys in the name or puppetry started to give way to a much stronger and more intense dream about one day becoming a performer like those singers and dancers I had seen on the stage.

I was consumed by the dream.

It was all I could think about, day and night.

At school, I started staging lunch-time productions with my friends in the back of the classroom, just so that I could in some small way attempt to realise what I was seeing in my mind's eye. But the back of the classroom was just the back of the classroom - it wasn't a stage. I yearned for more as my dream continued to grow, getting hungrier and hungrier with each passing day.

So every Saturday, to feed my dream, I convinced my Mum to let me catch the train by myself into the city so I could hang around in the QPAC foyers and just soak up the theatre atmosphere. If I couldn't be on the stage, I thought, then at least I could be in its vicinity. I just loved being at the theatre. I had no money to buy a ticket to see anything that was showing, but just mingling with audience members seemed to be enough to feed my little burgeoning dream's insatiable appetite. On more than one occasion, when everyone had gone in to find their seats, I found a discarded programme and sat outside by the banks of the Brisbane river pouring through it until the sunlight was fading and it was time to take the train home. Over the years, I amassed quite a collection of stolen programmes and became quite the musical theatre aficionado by gleaning information from those pristine glossy pages. I read the artist's biographies with great fascination and devoured the director's and producer's notes like they were food for my fantasies. My most beloved of all in my heaving collection was the programme for Simon Gallaher's landmark Australian production of *The Pirates of Penzance*.

I poured over that thing so regularly that it quickly became a tattered mess held together only by sticky tape and love. I read with awe and wonder about this entertainer-turned-entrepreneur Simon Gallaher who had produced the multi-million dollar Gilbert & Sullivan juggernaut that took Australia by storm in the early 1990's. I had no idea what a producer did, but in his programme notes he talked about growing up in Brisbane with big dreams and aspirations, and it dawned on me that I was growing up in Brisbane and I had big dreams and aspirations too. Something about the fact that this impresario came from the same part of the world as me got me thinking that maybe I could be successful someday too. *If Simon Gallaher could live in Brisbane and make his dreams come true,* I thought, *then maybe so could I.*

My dream grew six feet taller just at the thought.

By late primary school, my weekly trips into the city to stand in crowded theatre foyers reading stolen programmes just weren't enough anymore to feed my ravenous, growing dream. I wanted to be in the theatre again, sitting in the seats, watching an actual show. Theatre was my drug, and I needed another hit. I saw an ad on television announcing that *Jesus Christ Superstar* was playing at QPAC and I nagged my mother so relentlessly to buy us tickets to see it that she eventually caved and we all went off to see it as a family excursion. My Mother and my sisters were only vaguely bemused by the whole thing, but I was completely and utterly swept away. Two hours in the theatre just wasn't enough to take it all in. I think I counted every light in the lighting rig, marveled at the detail in every costume, and reveled in the music and the wondrous singing and the high-energy dancing. Every part of the production bore its way into my psyche – if my dream had been a flickering candle, then *Jesus Christ Superstar* was like a tank of gasoline that ignited my dream into a raging bonfire, and I came away feeling like I was literally bursting with inspiration.

Standing in a crowded foyer didn't cut it any more. It wasn't enough to sit in the theatre seats and watch a show. I had to let what was inside of me out. I had to unleash my inner creativity and bring my dream to life.

I had to get on the stage. I simply had to!

I began begging my mother to let me attend weekly drama classes. She was reluctant at first, mostly because our family was fairly religious and in church circles it was widely thought that a life in the theatre would "corrupt my innocent mind". Thankfully, Mum did some research and discovered that there was a church in the city that had started up a little community theatre company called Harvest Rain, and besides presenting plays, pantomimes and musicals out of their small theatre in New Farm, they had also begun running Saturday theatre classes for children. The fact that this little company was auspiced by a church gave Mum confidence that the teaching wouldn't lead me straight to the gates of hell. She signed me up and the very next Saturday my dear Mother bundled my two younger sisters and I into the car. We travelled across town en route to the Sydney Street Theatre in New Farm, where Harvest Rain's classes were held. I was bouncing in my seat with excitement the entire trip, a blazing inferno dream burning brightly inside me. As the car turned on to Sydney Street, I saw a big green tin shed flanked by magnificent fig trees, and the sign on the door welcomed us to Harvest Rain. From the outside, the building appeared to be some kind of disused warehouse, but once I stepped through the front doors I was greeted by a cosy foyer and beyond that a theatre with a seating bank with a few hundred seats and beyond that….a stage.

A real actual stage.

In a real theatre.

I could have died and gone to heaven right then.

Up until that moment, standing on a slightly raised podium at the local park or perching on a pillar at a shopping mall was the closest I had ever really come to being on a stage, and now, here I was on a legitimate theatre stage in a real actual theatre learning from real actors about how to really act. In my mind, I was the luckiest kid on earth; I was living the dream.

At last, I was on the stage!

I adored being around other children who loved being on that stage as much as me, and those two hours every Saturday while my

Mum and my sisters waited for me in the park down the street were absolutely pivotal and transformational for me, because at last, my insatiable dream was satisfied. I had fed it for so long, and it had grown so big inside me that now it had been forced out into my reality. It was not the last dream I would nurture in my mind – there would be many, many more dreams to feed – but the achievement of that small dream taught me that my dreams were worth pursuing, so I began to make space for a new dream to grow.

We all have a dream growing inside of us.

When we give that dream our time and our attention, it expands.

When we feed it, it grows.

Ignore it, and it festers.

Do not ignore your dreams.

Embrace them.

Cherish them.

Believe in them.

Don't let anyone tell you that your dreams are silly.

Don't believe others when they say your dreams are not realistic.

Dreams are not meant to be realistic.

Our dreams are meant to expand our reality, not conform to it.

You have a dream bubbling inside of you. Perhaps you've been paying it attention. Perhaps you've been ignoring it. Perhaps you forgot it was there all together and are only just remembering it now. Nonetheless, you have a dream.

It wants to grow.

It wants to live.

Your dream is hungry.

It's time to feed it.

## CHAPTER TWO
# THE BEAUTIFUL UNFOLDING

I always have a bunch of oriental lilies in a vase of water sitting on my kitchen counter.

Every week without fail, I take a trip down to my local flower shop to purchase a posy of my favourite flowers to rest delicately on my bench top. I always try to buy them as closed buds, because that way they last longer, and you also get to watch them slowly unfurl. One at a time, the little buds gradually spring open and gently their petals unfold ever so deftly until the whole bouquet is in full bloom. They're stunning to look at, and they fill the whole house with their striking aroma.

My love for lilies goes right back to my childhood when my Great Aunty Ellen used to keep a bunch of lilies on her kitchen counter the same way that I do now. Every time I visited her house, I would find myself transfixed by the flowers, mesmerised by their exquisiteness, and I always took great delight in studying each one to see how the buds were opening, and which ones were in bloom. One day when I was no more than five years old, I climbed up on to Aunty Ellen's kitchen counter and attempted to pry one of the closed buds open with my hands. My Aunt dove across the living room like a ninja to swat my hand away.

"Not now, Timothy," she said, gently guiding my hand away from the lily. "It has to open by itself. If you try to force the lily open, you will kill it, and you'll miss the beautiful unfolding".

Life is just like those lilies. You can't force it, you can't pry it open before its time. When dreaming big dreams for your life, you have to wait and be patient and allow those dreams to blossom and bloom into reality naturally. When we release our need for things to play out as we planned, according to our own timing and in our own way, we allow life to bring our desires to us just exactly as they should be, as life needs them to be, in exactly the right way in exactly the right moment, fully formed, perfect, better than we ever could have imagined.

That's the beautiful unfolding.

I'd been attending weekly youth theatre classes for a little over a year when one of my teachers pulled me aside after class one day and told me that Harvest Rain was producing a play that featured a role for a young boy and they wanted me to audition. I was ecstatic – coming to drama classes every weekend had really fueled my dream of one day becoming a performer, and now there was an opportunity to realise that dream, and I was only thirteen years old! The director came and auditioned me after class the following weekend. He explained that the play was called *Shadowlands*, a serious, dramatic piece about the life of C.S. Lewis, and the role I would be auditioning for would require me to cry on cue, which I'd never been much good at. Nonetheless, I squeezed out some tears, and the director seemed pleased enough that he ended up offering me the role.

Well, I thought I was just about the best thing since sliced bread.

I was only in about three scenes, but none of that mattered to me.

I thought I was Laurence freaking Olivier.

I felt like I had really made it.

News travelled around my school pretty fast that I'd "hit the big-time". I wandered around the place, feeling mighty pleased with myself and letting everyone know it. While the rest of my class would obviously have to continue on with their eighth grade studies, it was clear to me that I had reached the heights of fame and glory, and at any moment, Broadway would beckon once they heard of my incredible three-scene performance in this little production playing in a tin shed theatre in downtown Brisbane. My future was set. I was an actor now. No need to continue schooling. I'd be far too busy acting, as I was certain to be in high demand. Fame and fortune were surely just around the corner.

*Shadowlands* played for twenty performances in the summer of 1994. Audiences enjoyed it, a few critics came along and praised it, I managed to remember all twelve of my lines and deliver them in sequence each night....and then the show closed. And the set came down, and the lights went out, and the actors went home. And I went back to being just a regular eighth-grade kid.

Broadway didn't call.

Fame and fortune did not beckon.

This was not the plan.

I had naively thought that once I had broken into the industry, I'd just be able to stay there forever, and roles would simply fall at my feet, and it would be an endless stream of work and opportunity. But that wasn't the case. There just weren't that many jobs going, certainly not ones for inexperienced thirteen-year-olds, so I returned to school the following year feeling very lost. People would ask me what play I was going to be in next and I'd lie to them and say, "There aren't any roles that interest me at the moment". Truth be told, any role would have interested me. I would have played a piece of gum on Hamlet's shoe if someone had asked me.

I started panicking. My dream had come true so easily that first time; I hadn't even been trying to make it happen, it had just happened. I'd just been bumbling along at youth theatre classes, casually dreaming of one day becoming an actor. I had placed no pressure on the realisation of the dream. I had just dreamt it and then got on with it, like blowing on a dandelion and watching it dance away with the wind. I hadn't laboured over the dream, I hadn't worried whether it would come true. It had just come to me in its own good time. Now, making my dream come true again felt like an awful lot of hard work. I needed to just let go and trust, but in all my panic and worry, I stopped believing for the beautiful unfolding. Now I started dreaming and panicking, dreaming and trying, dreaming and demanding; placing pressure on my acting dream to come true again, now, now, now. Deliver the goods now, now, now, exactly as I want it, on demand, now, now, now.

But the more I pushed, the less it came.

The more I scrambled, the further away it seemed.

Not long after, my drama teacher at the Harvest Rain Youth Theatre fell pregnant, and classes were put on hold until she returned from having her baby (spoiler alert: she never returned!). So high school drama classes became my one and only opportunity to extend myself in the arts, and I milked every morsel of goodness out of those lessons like my life depended on it. I took it very seriously, partly because I saw myself as a very serious actor having been in a grand total of one production, but also because my drama teacher at school, Mr Burgess, was a very serious man and as such he encouraged us to take ourselves and our craft very seriously. He was tall and thin, towering over us all with his commanding presence and his somewhat threatening gaze. When he wasn't teaching at school, he ran his own theatre troupe, so in my mind, he was as legitimate as they came and I respected him as someone who really understood the arts and knew what he was talking about.

Kate was my best friend in drama class. She was sweet and kind, popular with everyone, and she loved acting just as much as me, although she was much better at it than I was because she had grown up going to dance school and singing lessons. Of course, I never admitted that at the time. We had a healthy competition going on in class – well, I competed with her, I don't think she felt any need at all to compete with me (when you're good, you just get on with it!).

One day, Kate came to me in the lunch hour.

"You know that show Mr Burgess is producing with his theatre troupe?" she said.

I pretended not to know much about it so as not to look desperate, but I was all over the details of that show like a rash. Mr Burgess' theatre troupe had adapted Calvin Miller's book *The Singer* into a full-scale musical, and they were preparing to stage the production for an interstate tour.

"Yeah, I think I've heard about it," I said, playing it cool.

"Well, apparently one of the lead roles needs to be played by a young girl, and so Mr Burgess has offered me the part!".

I'd love to say that I was instantly happy for Kate and that we hugged and jumped around and let off some streamers and wept tears of joy and celebration. But that wouldn't be true. I was immediately green with envy. I literally think I actually turned a little green, for real. Full Elphaba.

"Wow, that's great!" I said through gritted teeth and then ran away as quickly as I could so I could cry behind the toilet block.

*I'm the professional actor in this school,* I thought.

*That role should be mine.* (Never mind that they are looking for a little girl).

*How dare she take that role away from me! How could she do this to me?*

Instead of being happy for Kate, I was just deeply jealous. I wanted to be in that show so badly. I wanted to be in ANY show so badly.

*How am I going to watch Kate go off to rehearsals each week and then go and see her in the show and pretend to be happy when I'm really just so, so, so jealous!*

Oh my giddy aunt, I was selfish.

And dramatic!

That afternoon, I came home from school and threw myself down on my bed and cried. I felt so confused. Kate was living <u>my</u> dream. It felt so unfair, and I couldn't make sense of it. I lay on my bed for a good few hours, sobbing melodramatically into my pillow, before I finally pulled myself together and decided I had to let it go.

It did me no good to live in a state of jealousy and frustration that things weren't playing out exactly how I wanted them to.

I just had to let the lily unfold.

I went back to school the next day determined that I wasn't going to be jealous that Kate's "lily" had bloomed before mine. I was just going to be happy for her success. You know, like an actual good friend would be. I smiled as I listened to her talk about how exciting rehearsals were, and every time I felt a pang of jealousy flare up, I thought about those lilies on my Aunty Ellen's table and reminded myself that all of the buds unfurled their petals eventually. I just had to be patient and wait for my beautiful unfolding.

Turns out I didn't have to wait too long. That day at recess, Mr Burgess called me into his office and said that they were looking for some young guys to take on roles in the ensemble of *The Singer* and he wondered if I would be interested in taking part.

Is the Pope Catholic? HELL YES!

I didn't know a single detail about the show or about the role. I didn't know when the show was playing. I didn't know who was directing it. I didn't know anything, and I didn't care.

I was in a show!

The lily was in full bloom!

Twice a week, Kate and I would carpool across town with Mr

Burgess to a rehearsal studio on the south side of Brisbane where *The Singer* was being rehearsed under the direction of a passionate and enthusiastic young girl named Abi. Abi was a real visionary, a great leader, and an outstanding director with an unbelievable knack for putting together large scenes with lots of people, which stood her in good stead directing *The Singer* which boasted an ensemble cast of over 40 performers. Abi would come to rehearsals each day armed with well-prepared mud maps detailing where each person would move on stage, and she was also responsible for much of the writing of the show. To me, it seemed like there was nothing she couldn't do.

I was just in awe of her.

When I wasn't in the scenes that were being rehearsed, I loved sitting to the side and just watching Abi direct. I found it totally fascinating. The way she handled the actors, the way she spoke, the way she thought, the way she listened; to me, it was like a masterclass in directing, and for the very first time in my life, I started to appreciate what it was to be a director. Other than my life-long fascination with Steven Spielberg since I'd seen "E.T" as a child and discovered this marvelous man who made movies happen, I'd never considered the role of a Director before. I had never pondered the thought of sitting in the Director's chair, but something about the way Abi worked made me want to be just like her.

Eventually, it came time for the show to head off on tour through regional New South Wales. In all the excitement of rehearsals, I'd never thought to really ask much about how the tour would work, or where we'd be staying or how we'd be travelling or anything like that. Turns out that maybe I should have! When you counted up all the actors, crew members and musicians, there were seventy people in the touring company. We were travelling by bus, but the bus they had hired to transport us only just fit all seventy of us, with little spare room for our bags and belongings. So, we travelled along with us all kind of just piled on top of each other. It was an excellent bonding exercise, to say the least!

On the first day of the tour, we travelled for over twelve hours to get to Coffs Harbour, the first destination on tour. The bus dropped us off outside the theatre at 4pm, we all unloaded and filed into the theatre where we were put to work building the set for the show. It didn't matter if you were the flute player or the stage manager, the chorus boy or the star of the show, we all had to muck in to get that set bumped into the theatre. By 6.30pm, it was tools down so we could all get into costume, and then by 7.30pm, the curtain went up on our first performance. As the first notes of the overture played, to our shock and dismay we all saw that there were only five people in the audience, each of them looking very sheepish and lonely against the vastness of the empty theatre. It's not about how many people show up, I guess, but it's pretty weird when there are seventy people on stage and only five in the audience. It seemed utterly pointless, but we forged ahead nonetheless and gave it our best. The curtain came down at 10.30pm, the five audience members left, and we all set to work dismantling the set and packing it into the truck before dragging ourselves back to the tour bus at midnight. We were all looking forward to having a warm shower and crawling into a comfy bed, but we soon discovered that instead of staying in a nice hotel, we would be sleeping on the hard, wooden floor of the local community centre. After a terrible night's sleep, we were back on the bus by 7am the next day, ready to travel to the next city and repeat the process again.

It was a freaking nightmare.

Travelling, unloading, building the set, performing to empty houses, packing down the set, sleeping on the floor of the local church or youth hall.

By day three, we were all grumpy.

By day five, we were livid.

By day seven it was turning into *Lord of the Flies*.

We all stank because we hadn't showered or washed our clothes in days. We didn't know where we were – the tour took us to every backwater town in regional New South Wales that nobody had ever heard of before. We were starving, so occasionally the organisers would buy ten hot chickens from the local supermarket, and we would all devour them like wild animals. We regularly performed to houses of less than 30 people and often found ourselves sleeping on pews in nearby churches, or on mats in the local gym – anywhere that would take us in for the night! What a debacle!

By the time the tour mercifully came to an end, I was completely exhausted but strangely inspired. I had expected that *The Singer* tour would be a great opportunity to extend myself as a performer. But in allowing my life to unfold without pushing or prodding or forcing any outcomes, I discovered a whole other side to the world of theatre that I really never knew anything about, and would never have otherwise known to be interested in had it not been for that horrendous and life-changing tour. Watching Abi lead us as actors had ignited within me an intense interest in directing - I could kind of see myself doing what she did someday. The experience of building the set each day on tour and seeing the lights being rigged in each venue birthed a desire to understand more about the inner workings of how theatre went together (or how it fell apart!). I had gone into the experience with the singular dream of becoming an actor, but as I relinquished the reigns and allowed life to unfold without any tampering or meddling from me, I developed a strong appreciation for the process of creating theatre as a whole, not just the on-stage stuff. No matter how chaotic and disorganised the tour had been, my mind had been opened, and my vision had expanded as my life continued to beautifully unfold.

By the time *The Singer* tour came to an end, I was in tenth grade, and my school sent us all out on work experience for a week so we could get a taste of what being in the workforce was really like. My teachers suggested that I might like to try working in theatre administration, and that sounded better than working in a law firm or a medical centre for a week, so I agreed, and to my surprise, they found me a work experience position in the administration offices of Harvest Rain. With my interest in life behind the theatre scenes having been well and truly sparked by *The Singer* tour, I was eager to spend a week peering "behind the red curtain" at Harvest Rain.

I rocked up on the first day and was greeted by two big, hefty men whose size and presence would have been overbearing if it hadn't been for their warm smiles. They introduced themselves as Robbie, and David Parkin, the Artistic Directors of Harvest Rain, and they showed me all through the theatre and their offices and then demonstrated how to answer the phones and take bookings and sell tickets. At first, I was terrified of answering the phone, but after a few days, I really got the hang of it and discovered that I actually enjoyed selling tickets and managing databases and getting to know the inner workings of the theatre company. I started to understand how the theatre was made and what it took to produce a show and run a company. On my last day of work experience, I thought to myself, "If acting doesn't pan out for me, I could always work in the Harvest Rain office and take bookings and make the coffees". Little did I know…

Upon returning to school, we were due to start rehearsals for the annual class play, so Mr Burgess sat us all down at the end of drama class to announce the casting for the show. One by one, he called out the characters in the play and matched them to people in the class. All the main characters were assigned to people, but my name was not mentioned – a minor blow, but I was so eager to just be on stage again in any capacity I didn't mind taking a supporting role. Sadly, all the supporting roles were called out and still no mention of my name. Mr Burgess got right down to the very smallest roles in the show, and still, my name had not been called.

I had been completely forgotten, it seemed.

The bell rang, and the class was dismissed, and I gathered my things feeling rather shell shocked that I'd been so overlooked. Mr Burgess called me aside as I was leaving the classroom, and I had to bite my lip because I was so filled with emotions I thought that if I didn't, I might just burst into the ugly cry right there in front of him.

"You're not going to be an actor, Tim," he said to me, blunt as anything. "I know you think you are, but you're not."

I bit down on my lip harder. Why not just beat me over the head with a cricket bat, I thought.

"I've been watching you and seeing how you interact with everyone. People listen to you. When you speak, they pay attention. You'd be wasted as an actor."

Those words were hard to hear said out loud. I felt like he'd taken a lifetime of dreams and put them through the shredder, just like that.

I wanted to bawl my eyes out. I heard it as him saying I was not good enough to be an actor, and he was punishing me by giving me no role in the class play.

It seemed cruel.

I thought about punching him in the face.

"But I really want to act", I managed to spit out.

"I know you do, but I think you can do more," he assured me. "I think you're going to be a director. In fact, I'm so sure you're going to be a director that I want you to direct our class play. That's why I didn't reserve a role for you. I want you to be the director."

At that moment, I think time briefly stood still.

I was shocked.

I was delighted.

I was all of the things, all at once.

In an instant, I went from feeling absolutely despondent that he didn't think I was going to be an actor, to being absolutely elated that he was trusting me to be a director.

A director.

Just like Abi.

It sounded good to me.

It wasn't what I had expected. I don't think I would have asked for it. But when it unfolded before my eyes, it was perfect and right and well-timed and utterly beautiful.

And that right there is the power of letting go.

Of saying to the universe, "Here's what I think, now show me what you think". Of letting go of the need for things to play out as you intend and trusting that they will play out exactly as they should if you can just hold on and be patient. Of getting down off the kitchen bench and letting the lilies just do what they know to do.

There will be a beautiful unfolding.

And those lilies will delight and surprise you every time.

When you strangle the dream, you kill it.

When you hold it too tight, you crush it.

When you release it - when you let it go – you allow it to grow and flourish and evolve, and you allow space for the universe to respond, and to say, "There is more. Here, let me show you".

When you let it go, you discover that the universe has a dream for your life bigger than the dream you can dream for yourself. You learn that you don't want to be the one who articulates every tiny detail of how your dream will unfold – you want to be the one who is trusting enough to release your dream back to the universe, saying "Use me. Mould me. Shape me. Grow me. Take me where you will."

When you are strong enough to let it go, when you are brave enough to release, you will see your dream unfurl and evolve into something more exquisite than you can possibly imagine.

And then the real magic can begin.

## CHAPTER THREE
# THE POWER OF PAPER AND PEN

Remember that song the Spice Girls used to sing back when they were a big deal in the late '90s? That song where they kept asking what you wanted, what you really, really wanted.

It's possible that I may have sung it into my hairbrush in front of my bedroom mirror on more than one occasion in my teenage years.

I played "Wannabe" so many times on my Discman (under 25's - google it) back when I was finishing my last year of high school that the laser burned a scratch in the CD.

I don't need your judgement, here, okay.

I need your support.

I admit: I am a recovering Spice-aholic.

In my youth, I suffered from a terrible pop music addiction. If your song had a catchy hook and a sick beat, I was all about it. If it sounded like it had been autotuned within an inch of its life, that was my jam. Cheesy pop music was my religion, and in the late 90's, the Spice Girls were my spirit guides. When those girls sang from atop their lofty platform shoes, I pondered their lyrics like they were missives from Buddha.

What did I want?

What did I really, really want?

Turns out, I didn't really, really know.

Of course, I knew what I wanted for the next few minutes – I wanted a snack, I wanted a nap, I wanted to watch TV, I wanted to zigzag ah (anything to please my beloved Spices) – but when it came to long term stuff and the larger notion of what I wanted for my life, I was a little more sketchy on the details.

Now, you're probably thinking I'm a bit of a loon for taking a question posed in a pop song so seriously. So, go on, laugh it up. I find it funny now too. But growing up, pop culture was everything to me, and that wasn't the first time that a song or a movie or a teen magazine had triggered some deep psychological questioning in my young, adolescent mind.

"What do I want?", I would ponder as I sang like a Spice Girl into my hairbrush.

I knew I wanted to be happy, but what did that actually mean, I thought?

What did happy look like?

I knew it was something creative, but what exactly? I couldn't articulate it, not specifically. And I wanted to be specific, because I had heard that Ginger Spice Geri Halliwell had made a "cosmic wish list" when she was a teenager, itemising all of the things she wanted from life in the belief that the universe would receive those wishes as instructions and get about the business of making them come true for her. On one of those lists, Geri wrote that she wanted a number one hit on the British music charts, long before it was logical that she would ever be able to achieve that goal, and in the end, the Spice Girls saw nine of their songs go to the top of the charts in the United Kingdom. So, I thought, if it's good enough for Ginger Spice, it's good enough for Ginger Me, and I started working towards figuring out what I wanted to write on my own cosmic wish list. After all, how could I start working towards achieving my goals if I didn't even know what they specifically were? You have to know where you're going if you ever want to actually get there.

Putting pen to paper turned out to be a much tougher task than I had expected. For weeks on end, I would sit on my bed with paper in front of me and pen in hand, but for the life of me, I couldn't seem to muster the fortitude to splash any ink on the page. Each time I pressed the pen up against the paper to write, I would be filled with this immense feeling of dread and fear, as if what I was going to write was so unthinkable, so unbelievable, so laughable, that the world would erupt into fits of wheezing and chortling before the ink had even dried. It was as if I knew very clearly what I wanted, but there was a part of me that was afraid to let me fully know it, or hear it, for fear that I might accept it or agree with it, and then I might do it, and the doing of it would be scary and precarious, and I was protecting myself from the potential peril. I knew what I wanted, but I wasn't allowing myself to acknowledge it, let alone write it.

I think the fear mostly came from the fact that just about everything I wanted to do with my life had the potential to take me away from my home. Brisbane certainly wasn't the entertainment capital of the world, and everyone knew that if you wanted to work in the entertainment industry in Australia, you had to move to Sydney or Melbourne, and something about that just devastated me. I loved Brisbane. I loved Queensland. I loved my family and friends. I didn't want to have to leave just to do the thing that I loved. The thought of it literally broke my heart, and so every time I went to write on that page, something inside stopped me, because I didn't want to have to leave. I didn't want to go away. Six months passed, and still, I had nothing written on my goals list.

The day after I graduated high school, I was home alone and - with no assignments to complete or exams to worry about - I was embracing my new-found ability to lie about on the couch all day long. I turned the television on and started flicking channels until I stumbled across the midday movie, which on this fateful day happened to be *The Muppet Movie*, a childhood favourite of mine. I was just in time to catch the last ten minutes of the film, where Kermit, after being on the run from the villainous Mr. Hopper for most of the movie, confronts his opponent with one of my favourite monologues ever committed to celluloid. In it, Kermit talks about having a dream that's all about singing and dancing and making people happy, and that it's the kind of dream that gets better the more people he shares it with, and that he'd found a whole bunch of friends with the same dream, and that shared dream made them like a family.

I had seen this movie a gazillion times before and could recite the dialogue back to front from start to finish, but somehow on this particular day, it caught my attention differently and unusually. It was like it spoke directly to the part of me that was afraid to write on my cosmic wish list and convinced it to let up, just for a moment. It felt like a veil was lifted, and I could clearly see what I wanted to do.

I wanted to make theatre happen.

I wanted to make theatre happen in the city I loved.

I wanted to stay.

I wanted to create.

I wanted to gather friends who wanted to stay and create too, and I wanted to make a place where we all could do what we loved together.

I found my way from the lounge to my bedroom and snaffled up some paper and as my pen hit the page I started drawing a rough mud map of a building that I could see in my head; a building that could be a home to people like me who loved musical theatre, complete with dance studios and rehearsal rooms and offices and a working theatre.

It was a place that didn't exist, not yet at least, but I wanted it to exist. I could see it in my mind's eye, and I knew it was a place where my dreams could unfold.

The sketches and drawings gave way to words, and eventually I went from scribbling ideas for the building where my dream could become a reality, to actually drafting full sentences and, at long last, an answer to the question of what I really, really wanted began to form.

I wrote:

*"Well, school is done.*

*It's sad to finish, but I feel like now I'm finally free to get on with what I want to do with my life. Everyone's feeling so sad and lost about the end of school, but I think that's because they don't know what they want to do with their lives. I guess I've always known. The only thing I feel scared about is that now I have to go and actually do it.*

*I'm going to write down my plan so that I have something to look back on in years to come to prove I always knew I'd get there someday.*

*I'm going to stay in Queensland and run my own theatre company.*

*I'm going to produce musical theatre*

*I'm going to make a place where people who love musical theatre can perform and train and feel like they belong.*

*I'm going to make a difference.*

*I don't know how I'm going to do it, but I know it's what I'm going to do. I'm not going to give up. I will find a way.*

*And someday I'll look back on this and say, "See, I told you I said I'd do it"*

All these years later, I still look at that entry in my 1998 planner diary and can't quite believe that everything I wrote on that cosmic wish list has become a reality in the twenty years since I put pen to paper.

Turns out Ginger Spice really knew a thing or two, didn't she?

Not laughing at my pop addiction now, are you?

It just goes to show that there's something really powerful about putting pen to paper. I read the other day that scientists conducted a study on a group of university students; half were asked to take notes on a lecture by hand, and the other half were asked to take notes by typing them onto a laptop. It turned out that the students who took notes by hand were more readily able to recall the words they wrote than those who typed theirs on a laptop - physically shaping words and writing them down by hand actually helps us to remember them. The feel of a pen being gently manipulated to produce the tiny strokes of ink that make up words on paper is far more tactile than fingertips pressed against bits of plastic on a keyboard, so our body pays attention to them differently, and stores them differently, and recalls them differently, and believes them differently. I didn't know it at the time, but the act of physically writing down my dream in detail served to store the specifics of that dream indelibly in my mind. My body received the information as instructional. It wasn't just hopes and wishes and dreams being applied to paper – it was a blueprint for the future, and while my waking mind forgot about it after I wrote it, the details of what I wrote were imprinted on my inner being, stored in my inner mind, branded like a road map for the future all over the walls of my inner soul. I wasn't just articulating what I hoped to do; I was telling myself what was going to happen, documenting the next few chapters of my story, setting the agenda, laying tracks in front of the train. It was a cosmic wish list, but as it turned out, it might as well have been a step-by-step instruction manual for my inner being to follow. There is power in putting pen to paper. I know that for sure, and now whenever I am looking to the future, I am sure to write down what I want, not because I need it to play out exactly as I see it in my mind, but because the act of writing it down gives me a sense of direction. The act of committing your dream to paper takes it from being just a thought to being an action – it takes it from being in your head to being something that exists in the real world, even if it is just on paper for the time being. It's the beginning of your dream having life, and the most important step in the process of realising your vision.

I am not special.

I don't have a magical diary or a pen that makes dreams come true.

I didn't dream bigger or harder than the next person.

There's no reason why you couldn't do everything that I have done and more.

The key to making your dreams come true is being brave enough to face them and articulate in detail what they look like.

Say what you mean.

Don't be vague.

Don't be general.

Be specific.

Get down to the nitty-gritty.

Decide what you want, what you really, really want.

Write it down.

Draw it out.

Thrash it out.

Just get it out–out of your head and on to the page, because there is power in putting pen to the page when it comes to dreaming big. It forces us to look at what we're thinking, to read it back, to fully digest it, to see it written out, confirmed in writing. That's powerful. Don't underestimate the mighty power of the written word, and don't overlook how you can use it to your advantage.

It's time to muster the courage to take the lid off your favourite pen, find yourself a clean sheet of paper, and start committing your vision to the page.

It will clarify.

It will enhance.

It will streamline.

It will focus.

And most of all, it will be received by the energy of all things as a clear instruction for the future. As a mud-map of what is to come.

Put your pen to the paper.

Set a clear direction.

And then, onwards!

Ever on!

## CHAPTER FOUR
# CLOSED DOORS, OPEN WINDOWS

There's a line in *The Sound of Music* - right at the start of the movie just before Julie Andrews leaps through the streets of Salzburg clutching her carpet bag and guitar case - where Maria says that God always opens a window every time he closes a door.

I love that saying.

It speaks to the notion that there is always a way forward, always an escape hatch, that you shouldn't spend too long pounding on a closed door, but you should try a different way, look for a new direction.

It's not our job to pick the locks of doors that are bolted shut.

They're shut for a reason.

Go where the doors are opening.

That was pretty much my philosophy when I graduated high school. I had this big vision for what I was going to do with my life, but no clear way of actually making any of it happen, so I went where the doors were opening, trusting that I'd made my intention quite clear and the universe would (hopefully) deliver.

One door that never opened for me was the door to the

university. If I'm honest, I didn't try very hard to make it open. In fact, I pretty much nailed the door shut by neglecting to apply for any tertiary courses at all and taking a year off after finishing high school instead. These days, it's quite common for school leavers to take a "gap year" before committing to further study. But back in the late '90s, breaking the news that you were planning on taking a gap year was met with the same kind of horrified gasps that you might expect to hear after telling someone you were thinking of taking arsenic or eating a battery or something like that. It seemed that everyone was just expected to go straight from school to university; even if you didn't know what you wanted to study. You were encouraged to just start studying anything, so many of my friends ended up blindly enrolling in courses which qualified them to do nothing more than go on to study another course, and it all just seemed ludicrous to me. I couldn't do it. It's not that I have anything against university or higher education; I just have never been very good at being told how to do a thing. I'm not one for reading instruction manuals (you should see some of the wonky flat-pack furniture I've put together in my time without the aid of instructions), and I learn by discovery, not by being told. I made a very conscious decision to avoid university and enjoy some time without study or structure. After twelve years of 6am wake-ups to get to school on time each day, I reveled in the laziness of sleeping in until 1pm every day and dragging my pyjama-clad self out into the living room just in time to watch Oprah on television every afternoon. While the rest of my school friends were sitting in university lecture halls taking notes, I was on my couch eating two-minute noodles and getting life-education from the Queen of daytime television.

Now, that's my kind of university!

I wasn't completely lazy though - I took a job as a cleaner at a swanky apartment block in the city, earning a couple of hundred dollars a week vacuuming floors in the early hours of each morning. It was a good job because it was all over by 9am each day, which meant I had my days and nights free to pursue my dreams. By this point, I was pretty set on running my own theatre company one day, just like I had written in my diary. Somehow I had formed this idea in my mind that heading up an arts organisation was something you could only do once you were in your thirties or forties once you had made a name for yourself in the industry, so I was feeling a little stuck like I was treading water while I waited to grow old. I couldn't find an example of anybody who had become the head of a major arts organisation before their 21st birthday. I'd heard of a few people who had started out as actors when they were young, got a bit famous and then moved on to being directors before eventually going on to running their own theatre companies, and I figured it would be wise for me to try and follow their lead. I started thinking that I just needed to become as famous as possible as quickly as possible to rise up the ranks and eventually achieve my ultimate goal.

So naturally, I turned immediately to reality television.

Reality television was in its infancy at the time. It was such a new concept that I'm not even sure it had even been given the name "reality television" at that point, but it was taking over television sets from one side of the globe to the other. In Australia, the most popular program in this new "reality" genre was a show called *Popstars*, where cameras followed the process of putting together a manufactured girl band. Thousands of girls from all across the country auditioned for a place in the group. It was just like *Idol* or *X-Factor*, long before either of those shows had ever been thought of. We all sat around glued to our television sets every Sunday night, laughing at the tone-deaf people giving it their best shot, and squealing with delight as our favourite contestants were selected to be part of the five-piece girl band, which went on to take the country and the charts by storm under the moniker, *Bardot*. Naturally, given my love for all things pop, I was completely obsessed with this show. I watched every episode (and even taped most of them on Mum's VCR so I could watch them over again and again), I bought every single the band released, and I even lined up to meet the girls when they performed at the local Westfield shopping centre.

I wanted to be in *Bardot* so badly.

"If only I were a girl," I thought, "then I could have auditioned and got in the group and then it could have been me wearing all those plastic clothes and singing through a synthesiser!"

Well, you can imagine my excitement when the second season

of *Popstars* was announced, and this time they were looking to create a mixed boy-girl band. All my Christmases had come at once. I sincerely thought that this was my big break – this was my way to instant fame and notoriety, and once I had won a place in this manufactured pop group and everyone in the country knew my name, I'd have enough clout to start my own theatre company. The path seemed clear enough to me. The plan made perfect sense in my head, so I put all my energy towards preparing for the big audition. I fashioned together a make-shift pair of ridiculous Spice-Girl-esque platform shoes by gluing two pairs of sandals together and taping them to the bottom of some old boots that I owned. I dyed my hair bright blue (because obviously, it's easier to stand out in people's minds when your hair is the colour of toilet cleaner) and I bought myself an outfit made entirely of pleather and glow-mesh.

Yes, glow mesh. Get that visual image in your mind.

You're welcome.

Even by 1990's standards, I looked utterly ridiculous, but I thought I looked absolutely tremendous and was sure I would stand out from the crowd. Turns out, I did stand out from the crowd, but for all the wrong reasons. After waiting in line for three hours, I finally got to sing eight bars of "American Pie" for the judges, but almost as soon as I opened my mouth, they quickly dismissed me, and I was ushered out the door. Clearly, my outfit had not turned their heads, and my singing skills weren't as prodigious as I had first thought. To add insult to injury, when the second series of POPSTARS eventually went to air, my audition featured in the segment where they made fun of all the dreadful people who tried out; I was sandwiched in between an outrageous drag-queen and a tone-deaf lady in spandex. It was humiliating – I was a laughingstock on national television.

Clearly, this was not the plan.

SLAM.

That door closed rather swiftly and definitively.

Not to worry, I thought. There were plenty of other doors to try.

A new door presented itself quite promptly when I heard that Harvest Rain was holding auditions for their upcoming production of *Joseph and the Amazing Technicolor Dreamcoat*. Even though I had no formal singing or dancing training, for some reason I felt quite certain that the lead role of Joseph was destined to be mine and that this would be the ticket to stardom and notoriety I thought I'd need to one day establish my own theatre company. So I began rehearsing my rendition of the song *"Close Every Door"* in my bedroom incessantly to the point where one day a neighbour in a house a few doors down the street hung his head out the window and screamed, *"I'll close the damn door if you'll just stop singing!"*. Undeterred, I went along to the auditions, a little nervous but quietly confident. When I got to the big green tin shed that was the Sydney Street Theatre, I was greeted by a friendly fellow named Peter Laughton, who was the Music Director, and Robbie and David Parkin, all of whom I had become friendly with during my work experience stint years earlier. They all smiled warmly at me and listened intently as I sang and gave my very best Jason Donovan impersonation, and then they thanked me politely and before I knew it the audition was over.

Later that week I got a phone call from Robbie Parkin.

"I'm sorry," he said, "but unfortunately we weren't able to find a role for you in this production."

I was devastated.

I thought the coat of many colours had my name on it, but now it seemed my Technicolor dream was dying. I didn't know what to say. I almost dropped the phone. I wasn't even good enough to get a role in the back of the chorus? I'd been singing *"Close Every Door"* for weeks, and now it felt like every door really was closing.

I was an actor without anything to act in.

I was a pop star who just didn't pop.

I had hedged all my bets on landing the lead role in *Joseph*. Now, what would I do? I couldn't just sit on the couch watching Oprah all day for the rest of my life.

How would I stay connected to the world of theatre?

How could I make a name for myself so I could go on to someday start up my own theatre company?

Luckily for me, Maria Von Trapp actually did know what she was talking about – a window really did open just as it felt like all the doors were slamming shut.

"We really want to keep you involved with the company," Robbie told me, obviously sensing my disappointment. "We'd be really happy for you to help out behind the scenes if you're interested."

Initially, my ego flared up, and I wanted to tell Robbie that working behind the scenes was beneath me artistically; I was a serious actor, not a stagehand. But then I realised that nothing is beneath you when you're at the bottom of the pile, and I was literally at the very bottom of the bottom, having basically done a grand total of jack squat in the theatre industry at that time. I decided that doing something was better than doing nothing, and I took Robbie up on his offer and leapt through that open window.

I started attending rehearsals and assisting the *Joseph* production team, mostly by sorting out sheet music, making coffee and taking notes. Eventually, I became involved with the costume department and helped out by embellishing costumes and headpieces (and by embellishing, I mean I attacked them with a glue gun, safety pins and gaff tape, which was about the extent of my costume making skills). Soon enough I moved on to prop making and helped to paint the set, and I ended up quite enjoying things on the other side of the red curtain as it gave me a chance to watch from the sidelines and further develop my understanding of exactly how a show came together.

I was struck by how Robbie led the production team, encouraging them to always be patient with the actors and careful with their words and attitudes. There were never any raised voices, even when things got stressful – just always a sense of calm and kindness that filtered down from Robbie through to the entire cast and crew. One day, when I was taking notes during rehearsals, I asked Robbie how he stayed so calm in such high-pressure situations. He said to me, "The way you get where you're going is just as important as actually getting there. The process should be as good as the product. No point having a great show if everybody hates and disrespects each other. If you look after the people, then the show will look after itself!" I liked that sentiment a lot, and as each day went on, I felt more and more drawn to the company and the people running it. I wanted to be there, I wanted to learn, I wanted to be part of the inner workings. I began to feel very deeply connected to Harvest Rain.

Around that time, the Parkin brothers called a mysterious Sunday afternoon meeting at the Sydney Street Theatre and invited all those of us who had been involved with Harvest Rain over the years to be in attendance. None of us knew why we were being summoned, but gladly accepted the invitation to all be together under one roof – actors, directors, stagehands, musicians; we all gathered in the stalls of the Sydney Street Theatre and listened intently as Robbie and David explained the purpose of the meeting.

"We are all very proud of Harvest Rain's success," David began, "and that we've been able to create so many wonderful theatrical memories here in this building over the years."

His voice quivered, and it became clear that both he and Robbie were emotional about what they had to say.

"As you all know, the church has always been a great champion of this company since it was formed by the congregation many years ago," Robbie intervened. "The church has always overseen all of the theatre company's operations and finances, but over the last few years, the theatre company has grown almost as large as the church itself, and the eldership now feel that it's time for Harvest Rain to branch out and exist as its own entity, separate from the church."

There was an audible gasp from the crowd that was gathered. We all knew that the church had recently gone through a change in leadership, and this sounded like Harvest Rain was being evicted against its will, which turned out to be not far from the truth. For many years, Robbie and David had both been pastors at the church, and part of their pastoral duties had included overseeing the theatre company. This proposed separation from the church, they explained, would see them both lose their jobs by the end of the year.

"The church leadership has graciously allowed us to take the name Harvest Rain as we leave and apply it to a new not-for-profit arts organisation that we intend to incorporate, so the company can continue, albeit with a different formal structure. And the church has said they will allow us to hire the Sydney Street Theatre so we can continue presenting our shows here."

The news wasn't all bad, but for some reason, it felt ominous. It wasn't the end of Harvest Rain, but things were clearly changing, and there was a great sense of trepidation and uncertainty amongst those of us who were in the room. The brothers explained that they had leased a small office space just around the corner from the Sydney Street Theatre that would become Harvest Rain's administrative headquarters effective immediately. They were asking for volunteers to help them man the front desk, answer phones and take bookings as they went out on a limb running their own company away from the protective umbrella of the church that had bolstered the company's operations since its inception almost two decades earlier.

I stuck my hand up straight away.

I wanted to volunteer in the new Harvest Rain office, and I wanted to do everything I could to ensure that Harvest Rain continued to thrive amid this difficult transition. I felt somehow attached to the company – this is where I had first found my feet as a young actor in the youth theatre, and where I had first felt validated as a creative person. This company was precious to me – it felt like my second home – and I wanted to be part of ensuring it continued to grow and prosper. I started making daily trips into New Farm each morning after finishing at my cleaning job so I could spend the day answering phones, taking bookings and generally trying to help out in the new Harvest Rain office however possible.

The new office was a tiny little shop front just around the corner from the Sydney Street Theatre in New Farm, just big enough to house three desks; one for Robbie and another for his brother David and a third where box office volunteers like me were stationed. This was in the days before computers really became a common thing, so there were no emails to reply to, no social media to manage, no website to update and no online bookings to process. My job was just to sit there all day answering phone call after phone call, taking down credit card numbers by hand, writing up credit card payment forms to take to the bank, and then writing details of each booking into this giant A3-sized thick-as-a-phone-book ticketing tome. I didn't get paid a cent, but I didn't mind. I really liked the office environment and the organisation of it all, plus the experience of actually working in the world of theatre felt exhilarating to me, even if I was just taking bookings. And I knew that I was helping to keep the company I loved so much alive and thriving, and that felt deeply meaningful and important to me.

As the days and weeks wore on, I started to use my time in the Harvest Rain office to extend myself in other areas and grow my understanding of how theatre worked and how to run a theatre company. I figured all that knowledge would come in handy someday, especially if I eventually wanted to run a company of my own. I'd often wait until David was out for lunch and then I'd hack into his computer and open his files containing the designs for company marketing material. I taught myself to use graphic design software by trawling through his files and seeing how he had created various pieces of artwork, and little by little (unbeknownst to anyone else) I became somewhat of a self-taught graphic designer.

I also tried to create systems in the office to make things run more smoothly, particularly in relation to the ticket booking process. The Parkin brothers had made a habit of diverting the office phone to their mobile phones after hours so as not to miss a single patron's call. This meant that if you phoned up to book a ticket over the weekend there was a good chance you'd end up chatting with David while he was brushing his teeth, or talking to Robbie while he was cooking his dinner. Then each morning, the brothers would leave scraps of paper on the front desk with booking details scribbled down on them so that I could transfer the information into the archaic paper booking system. More often than not, the contact phone number would be illegible, or the credit card payment details were wrong, or the booking name was indecipherable, and on one occasion, David handed me booking information scrawled on a piece of toilet paper. I don't even want to think about where he was when he took that booking, or what the customer on the end of the line may have been hearing while handing over payment information. It seemed like a really chaotic system to me, so I gently encouraged the brothers to avoid taking bookings on scraps of paper after hours anymore.

"Our patrons expect to be able to make a booking any time of the night or day," David said to me in protest.

"That's only because you've taught them that they can," I postured. "Let's start handling the phones from 9am to 5pm on weekdays, and then leave a detailed after-hours message on the phone system encouraging callers to either call us back or leave their details, and we'll get back to them." I was all for looking after the patrons, but taking their calls 24-7 just didn't seem practical or necessary, I thought.

"This company only exists because of the people who buy tickets to see our shows. We wouldn't be here without the people," David reminded me. "Never forget that".

He was right. Over the previous fifteen years, the Parkin brothers had built up a remarkable rapport with their audience and had a real heart for the Harvest Rain patrons as people and individuals, not just ticket buyers. They weren't just "bums on seats" to the Parkins. They really, genuinely cared for their audience, even more so now that there was no church to auspice the company and the brothers' ability to earn an income relied heavily on patrons buying tickets. So, in the end, I resigned myself to the fact that if the brothers wanted to take bookings at midnight at home in their beds, then who was I to stop them?

By the time I was 20 years old I had managed to become somewhat of a permanent fixture in the Harvest Rain office, still volunteering and working for free, but I didn't mind the lack of remuneration because I felt like I was getting on the job training. I was learning more than I ever could have from a textbook or a university lecture. I'd started out with a clear goal to make myself famous so that I could use that fame to start my own company, but every way I tried to implement that plan had failed miserably – every door I tried slammed shut in my face. Life forced me to look in new and different directions; it used the closed doors to direct my path. I started realising that sometimes not getting what you want actually leads you to something that you want even more. And I began to understand that it wasn't just any company that I wanted to run someday.

It was Harvest Rain.

I wanted to be at the helm of Harvest Rain.

I didn't want to have to go out and build something from scratch, because what I thought I wanted to build already existed in the form of Harvest Rain.

No point building it twice.

So I decided I would find a way to stay around, find a way to further attach myself to the company, ingrain myself in its inner workings, be in the right place at the right time every time so that I could become an integral part of steering the company and moving it forward. It felt like the perfect place to be. I had simply walked through the open door and what lay on the other side turned out to be an opportunity that was better and more perfect than anything I could have expected.

When you venture out towards your dreams, you will invariably meet roadblocks along your journey. Never let those roadblocks get you down. They don't come to stop you, but to steer you. They are a gentle way of nudging you in a slightly different direction. They are a subtle prodding, encouraging you to look over there at that thing you would never have considered had you not met the roadblock in the first place. Closed doors are not dead ends, but rather markers or pointers along your travels, guiding you in exactly the way you need to go to get to the best the universe has for you.

Don't begrudge the closed doors.

Don't spend too long tugging at them or trying to pry them open.

Look for the open window.

Look for the door left slightly ajar.

There is always another way, and usually, it's better.

When one door closes, another always opens, and if you can be brave enough to walk through it and onwards to the next door and the next door and the next and the next, you will discover that everything you want and everything you desire lies just beyond those open doors and windows.

# CHAPTER FIVE
# CHOOSE YOURSELF

The thing about dreaming is that it's a fairly passive activity; the actual act of dreaming doesn't get an awful lot done. Dreaming sets the goal and lays out a road map for the future, but at some point, you have to get up off your butt and actually start walking the road.

It's not going to walk itself.

Sometimes, beginning the journey is the hardest part. The road ahead looks so long and winding, it makes the idea of just staying home and continuing to dream look deeply enticing. Sometimes, the trouble is that you just don't know where to start; You know where you want to get to, but you're not sure where to begin, or you take a few steps and suddenly don't know where you are in relation to where you want to go. Navigating the path from dream to reality can be quite an unpredictable rollercoaster.

It had been three years since I finished high school, which meant it had been almost three years that I had been volunteering in the Harvest Rain office, working on the front desk every day, unpaid, helping the Parkin brothers keep the company afloat now that it was no longer an arm of the church. The process of separating from the church and setting Harvest Rain up as its own entity had proven to be fairly challenging. Before the split, Harvest Rain had never been required to pay its own bills or rent or wages – all of that had been taken care of by church management. Now, it was up to the Parkin brothers to find the money required each week to pay the rent for the new office space and to fund the various productions the company was mounting. With no government funding or philanthropic support, the company relied entirely on ticket sales to make ends meet. It was a real baptism of fire for the brothers and for all the members of Harvest Rain's newly formed board of directors, all of whom were passionate about seeing Harvest Rain continue, but mostly in the dark about exactly how to manage and operate a fledgling independent arts organisation.

In the early days of the newly formed company, both the Parkin brothers took a wage from the company and worked in the office every day. As the months wore on it became apparent that this fledgling organisation couldn't sustain two full-time employees, so the brothers had to go out and find other jobs in order to be able to afford to keep food on the table for their families. Robbie started driving a taxi for some extra income and would often swing by the office mid-shift to check how things were going, and Dave took freelance graphic design work wherever he could find it. Ultimately though, on most days, I was the only person in the office. It was a completely bizarre situation; this big renowned theatre company was being run from day to day by a lowly volunteer.

It must have been a horrible time for the Parkins, scrambling to keep everything at Harvest Rain afloat while also scrounging for the dollars to pay their mortgages and put food on the table. I didn't have any of that stress. I was young and still lived at home, so I could afford to come in and man the office each day for free to keep the company's wheels turning. After a while, though, the grind started to get to me. I began to feel like I was treading water. Not doing much beyond reception duties, I was conscious of the fact that all my school friends who had gone off to university were now graduating with degrees and getting proper jobs and earning good money. Meanwhile, I was still volunteering for this little theatre company and not getting paid. Sometimes I questioned if I was making wise decisions by devoting so much of my time to holding down the fort in the Harvest Rain office, when I could have been off earning a degree and getting a job. I'd tie myself up in knots thinking like that, and then I'd pinch myself and take stock of the incredible opportunity that was unfolding in front of my eyes. By volunteering at Harvest Rain I had the luxury of being able to involve myself in whatever part of the company I liked, grow my skills in whatever area I chose and extend myself however I felt was most necessary for both my own development and the needs of the company. I was getting a free education – on the job training – and I loved it. Even though I was working without pay and most of my friends thought I was wasting my time, I started to see that I was being given a chance to back myself and choose my own way, carve my own path towards a future that would look the way I wanted it to. For someone who never liked being taught how to do things and who preferred to figure things out for himself, my life was panning out pretty perfectly.

In the summer of 2001, it was decided that the company's next production would be the classic musical *Oliver!*. The Harvest Rain board appointed a director to the show, as well as a choreographer and a music director, but it soon became apparent that nobody had been put in charge of actually running the production. Who would organise the auditions, notify actors of casting, type up and distribute rehearsal schedules, and things like that, I wondered? I looked around the office for an answer, but nobody else was there, so I decided I'd just have to do it myself. It was time that I took a little more initiative and responsibility, I thought. Since I was the one holding down the fort each day, I figured it was up to me to start calling the shots on how things were done on a day-to-day basis.

When it came time for the *Oliver!* auditions, hundreds of children turned up to try out, and just over sixty of them were selected to play the orphans in the show, alongside thirty adult performers. It was a huge group of people to manage and an awful lot of children!

"Who's going to look after all these kids backstage?" I asked one day when Robbie stopped in at the office in-between cab shifts. "They can't just be left to their own devices!"

"Maybe you can look after them?" he suggested, running out the door, and so I suddenly went from being Production Co-Ordinator to also being King of the Kids.

Every Saturday when the cast would come together for rehearsals, it was my job to monitor all sixty children, keep in touch with their parents, deal with any injuries, monitor behaviour and generally try and keep order with the junior members of the cast, whilst also making sure the rest of the production was running to schedule. The director and the choreographer didn't really see eye to eye, so I often found myself having to be the buffer between them. There wasn't a lot of cohesion amongst the creative team, and as a result, we were always running behind schedule, which meant actors who had been called in for specific times ended up sitting around all day doing nothing. It drove me slightly mental, but I held my tongue and just tried my best to keep things running smoothly in the background and smile while I was doing it.

There were some great people on that show who made the experience enjoyable. Peter Laughton was serving as the music director on the show, and we'd always got on well ever since he'd auditioned me for *Joseph*. He'd become a great friend who was always good for a laugh and having him there made the long hours somewhat bearable. One day, he sidled up to me during a break in rehearsals.

"You're doing a great job at keeping everyone in line," he said with a smile.

"Someone's got to do it," I said, through somewhat gritted teeth.

"Is this what you want to do - work in production?" he asked.

"Well, yeah, kind of," I replied. I leaned in close and whispered, "I'd love to do some directing someday."

"Directing?" Pete mused. "I think you'd make a great director."

"Really?" I replied.

"Well, a director has to know what he wants," Pete smiled, "and you clearly know what you want."

It was nice to hear that vote of confidence from someone I respected so much.

As we moved into the theatre and edged closer and closer to opening night, things became more and more chaotic. Rehearsals frequently ran over time, and I constantly had to remind the director that the children would have to leave at their agreed finish time or the parents would start a riot. I felt it was important we stick to the schedule, for the sake of the kids and their long-suffering parents.

During performances, the children were held in an upper room backstage at the Sydney Street Theatre, and I was put on duty keeping them focused and energised. It was a big show for them, and many of them were only eight years old and experiencing the immense high of being on stage for the very first time. A lot of the kids in that production have gone on to have really successful careers in the entertainment industry - Jack Chambers went on to win *So You Think*

*You Can Dance*, Mark Hill became a NIDA graduate and starred in a swag of musicals, Zahra Newman forged a stellar career both on stage and in films playing opposite the likes of Cate Blanchett, and Callum Mansfield became one of Australia's most sought after choreographers (and my best friend as well!) - but back then, they were all just a bunch of rag-tag kids, more interested in mucking around in the dressing rooms than anything else. But no matter how rowdy they got backstage, they always pulled out a great performance on stage, and I felt like a proud big brother to them all!

The happy, friendly atmosphere of our little upper room was shattered one night during intermission when a senior member of the creative team stormed backstage and really ripped into the children. He seemed furious, and he let the kids have it.

"You guys sucked!" he bellowed at the children as they huddled in the dressing room. "You ruined the whole first act. You're not focused, you're just mucking around. You all totally sucked!"

He just kept shouting at them over and over again while I stood there, wide-eyed and in shock. Anger bubbled up inside me. This just wasn't right, I thought. Taking out your frustrations on a bunch of little children, demoralising them and embarrassing them when they had all just been trying their best, was simply beyond the pale, in my opinion. When his tirade ended, and he finally left the room, I gathered all the kids together and apologised to them for his behaviour. I made sure they all knew that what he had said was inappropriate and not true. They didn't suck. They were some of the most hardworking kids I'd ever come across.

Even though an official apology was made to the children the following night, I still felt angry. I still felt mad. When you are given a senior role and a responsibility like that, you shouldn't squander it or abuse the position. I would have killed to be on that creative team, I thought, and if I was given an opportunity like that I felt sure that I wouldn't tell any children that they sucked. I started feeling really bitter about the whole scenario, like I was putting everything on the line to help keep Harvest Rain afloat, but being overlooked and not really reaping many benefits for myself. I didn't really want to be answering phones all day and taking bookings, and drafting schedules and wrangling children all my life.

Ultimately, I wanted to be on the creative team.

I wanted to direct.

I wanted to produce.

And I knew I could nail it if I was just given a chance.

"When will it be my turn?" I moaned to my mate Terri one day after work. "I've been volunteering there for three years keeping everything running smoothly, and the directing gigs go to everyone but me! It's not fair!"

Terri was seven years older than me, and almost my complete

opposite; she was a smoking, drinking, foul-mouthed atheist and I was a straight-laced, wide-eyed goody-two-shoes, but somehow we just clicked and got along. We'd met years earlier performing in a Harvest Rain show, and ever since I'd formed the habit of stopping by her house most days after work, and while she sat on the front deck of her flat smoking cigarettes I'd sit inside trying to avoid inhaling the second-hand smoke, and we'd talk through the fly screen door for hours and hours, never running out of conversation. Terri understood me, and I understood her.

"You have to be patient," Terri said bluntly. "You're only young. Your time will come."

"But when?" I whined. "How much longer do I have to wait?"

"Don't wait," Terri replied. "Stop waiting for them to be impressed by you. Stop waiting for them to choose you. Choose yourself. Put on your own show. Back yourself. Then they'll see."

Terri was right. I was such a people pleaser, and I was working my butt off in that office in the vain hope that the Parkin brothers would notice and pat me on the head and give me a gold star and say "Thank-you, here's a show for you to direct". It just wasn't going to happen that way.

"You're right!" I declared. "We should put on our own show."

"We?" Terri queried.

"Yes, why don't we?"

My mind was whizzing at a million miles an hour. I think big by default, and when an idea comes to me that I like, I latch on to it and don't let go.

"*Jesus Christ Superstar!*" I blurted out.

"I beg your pardon?" Terri said with a confused look.

"*Jesus Christ Superstar,*" I repeated. "I reckon we could totally pull it off. I'll direct, you can choreograph – it'll be awesome".

Terri smiled at me, the way I'm sure nurses smile at escaped mental patients as they coax them back into their padded cells.

"Don't you think *Jesus Christ Superstar* is a bit of a big undertaking for your first venture as a producer?" she postured.

"Fair enough," I relented. "Maybe we could just start off with a small little cabaret and work our way up to *Superstar*".

"But how?" Terri said. "We don't have any money!"

"We wouldn't need much money," I said, not really knowing what I was talking about. "Just enough to hire a theatre for a weekend. We could throw together a little cabaret show and charge our friends to come and see it. How hard could it be?"

The whole concept of producing our own show seemed overwhelming to Terri, but it really energised me. Every day I'd sit on

Terri's couch imploring her to take the leap with me until eventually, my enthusiasm wore her down, and she came up with a suggestion for the kind of show we could create.

"I was in this show a few years ago," she told me "where the whole thing was completely controlled by the audience. I think we could do something like that".

She went on to explain that her theatre mentor at university – an eccentric theatre maker named Jeanne-Pierre Voos - had created this show where the actors had a set series of tasks to complete that they could only carry out at the behest of the audience. The audience were given a set of musical instruments – a maraca, a woodblock, a triangle and so forth – and each instrument correlated to an actor on stage, so as each actor heard their instrument being played, they would carry out their first task then wait to hear their instrument being played again before moving on to their second task and so on. If the audience was clever enough, they could cause the actors' tasks to intercept, or they could leave an actor stuck in a task for a prolonged period, or they could leave the actor doing nothing at all, depending on what they wanted to see. Terri told me that the first task she had to complete when she heard her instrument was to put on tap shoes and start tap dancing, and she couldn't stop until she heard her instrument being played again. Apparently one night, she was left tap dancing for fifteen minutes straight with no rest. It sounded like torture, but also really innovative and fascinating; carefully orchestrated but also entirely random depending on what the audience wanted to see.

"Tez, let's do it!" I said, eager to get cracking.

"I'll have to call Jeanne-Pierre first and ask him if we can borrow his concept."

She made the call, and Jeanne-Pierre graciously allowed us to borrow the idea, and so *The Randomania Show* was born, based on a concept by an eccentric Frenchman, built by a determined out-of-work actress and ushered into reality by an eager twenty-year-old with a desire to make things happen.

Over the coming weeks, Terri set to work writing and plotting and scheming for *The Randomania Show*, coming up with the most ingenious sequences that would allow the audience to control how everything played out on stage. After weeks of writing, we had the bare bones of a show and were ready to cast the five characters that Terri had written. Naturally, Terri and I intended to be in the show, so we took two of the roles, and then we invited our friends Scott, Laurel and Kym over to play the other three parts. They all came around to Terri's place one night, not really knowing what they were in for, and Terri laid out the vision for the show, and a reading of her witty little script ensued. We all immediately knew that what Terri was writing was incredibly special, deeply clever and intensely original, and we were eager to bring the whole thing to life.

Through my time volunteering at Harvest Rain, I'd become friendly with the people who owned the Sydney Street Theatre, so I put in a call to them and inquired if they had any availability for us to put on our show there. There was a week free in September, and I took a pencil booking immediately! I did a rough budget in my head and worked out that if the theatre cost $1,000 to hire for a week, then we'd have to consider sound and lighting hire costs, printing of flyers, props, sets and costumes, so the whole thing would cost in the vicinity of $5,000 to produce. If we sold tickets for $30 each, we'd need 170 people to see the show to cover our costs. It seemed fairly achievable to me, but when I laid out the maths for Terri, she flipped out.

"We don't have five thousand dollars!" she pointed out.

"But we don't need it all up front," I explained to her. "We can pay the theatre rent from the ticket sales, and the same with the flyer printing costs and the sound and lighting hire. It's just the set, props and costumes that we'll need to pay for up front. I reckon we'd only need a thousand dollars."

"But we don't have a thousand dollars!" Terri pointed out again. She was smoking heavily by now, and she was right. We were both flat broke and had no way of coming up with $1,000 any time soon, so in the end, we decided it just wasn't possible to proceed.

"I'll call everyone in the morning and tell them it's off". Terri said, before turning in for the night.

I remember driving home from Terri's place that evening and

feeling so despondent. We had such a good idea for what would be a really incredible show, and it was never going to see the light of day because of money.

Stupid money!

The next morning, Terri called me on the phone.

"You won't believe it," she blathered down the line. "I rang Kym to tell her the show was off, and when she asked the reason why and I told her we didn't have enough money, she offered to loan us a thousand bucks!"

We couldn't believe our luck! The show could go ahead, thanks to Kym's unexpected and overwhelming generosity. Her willingness to put her own money on the line was such a vote of confidence and one of the most genuinely touching acts of kindness I had ever known. With her financial backing, we were able to put the wheels in motion and start the journey towards opening night.

Twice a week and all day on Sundays, we'd congregate in Terri's living room, push the sofa to the side and clear a space for rehearsals. With me handling the producing duties and Terri overseeing the direction and choreography, we started cobbling the show together, scene by scene, and before long we had a full 90-minute show, complete with five song-and-dance numbers and a whole series of audience controlled sequences. In no time at all, September came and opening night was upon us, and I remember the feeling of elation when I peeked out through a hole in the set and saw that people had actually turned up to see our show. The theatre was packed! The audience roared with laughter at our show – in one particular sequence, when I heard my instrument played, I had to go to the corner of the stage and crack eggs over my head until the audience moved me on. On that first night, the audience was having such a good time that they left me there to crack three whole cartons of eggs over my head. It was disgusting and awesome! I sang and danced my way through the rest of the show completely covered from head to toe in egg yolk, and at the end of the night, the audience exploded into rapturous applause, which continued long after we left the stage. Terri and I stood in the dressing room and listened to the hooting and hollering, overwhelmed and relieved that it had all worked out.

After the show that night, we went to the box office and discovered we'd sold enough tickets to not only pay back Kym's $1,000 loan but also to cover all of our costs. It felt like a miracle – we had put on a show and we'd made it pay!

In a matter of months, I'd gone from being that kid volunteering at the Harvest Rain front desk waiting for someone to give him a chance, to being the producer of a runaway hit show that people all over town were talking about and clambering to get tickets to. I'd never felt satisfaction like it.

I wasn't waiting to be chosen any more.

I had chosen myself, and it felt good.

A few days after our closing night, the phone rang, and it was Peter Laughton, calling to congratulate me on the success of the show.

"You guys did a great job," he said. "It's not easy putting on your own show."

"You're telling me," I said with a laugh.

"You deserve more opportunity to show what you can do," he said. "At the last Harvest Rain board meeting, I managed to convince the Parkin brothers to let me direct the company's next musical, and I think that you should co-direct it with me."

What now? Say that again?

"They probably wouldn't take a chance on you directing by yourself because you're so young," Pete explained, "but if we co-direct, then they really can't say no. Terri should be involved too. All three of us! What do you think?"

It was completely surreal.

The thing I had wanted to happen had finally happened. I was being given a chance to direct, to stretch my legs creatively, flex my directorial muscles and show everyone what I could do (or at least, what I hoped I could do!). To me, this was huge, and I felt immensely grateful to Pete for his faith in me, and for standing in the gap on my behalf. I hardly knew what to say, so I just said:

"Sounds great Pete. Thank-you. I'd love to."

I was lost for words, so much so that I almost forgot to ask Pete the most important question of all.

"What's the show we'll be directing?" I asked.

"Oh, you'll love it," he said. *Jesus Christ Superstar.*"

These days when I'm working with young actors or mentoring up and coming performers, the thing I tell them most often is "Never wait to be chosen". You have to back yourself before anyone else will back you. When you believe in yourself, you set the example for others, and you literally teach people how to feel about you by the way you feel about yourself. If you hold yourself back, waiting for others to believe in you, waiting for others to back you and offer you an opportunity, you could be waiting a long time. But when you get moving, when you back yourself, when you step out in faith and start making stuff happen for yourself, people take notice. The universe takes notice. It reads to others like an invitation, saying "I see myself up here; come on up and meet me".

Parked cars are hard to steer – it's much easier to maneuver a moving vehicle. Likewise, people who sit on their couch dreaming their whole life but never actually rising up and trying towards their dream end up getting nowhere.

You have to move.

You have to act.

You have to get going.

Don't wait for the moment - make the moment.

Don't wait for other people's backing - back yourself.

Get on with it.

Get going.

Get moving.

It doesn't matter so much which direction you go in, what matters is that you go. Once you're moving, then you can steer. Once you're on your way, then the universe can gently guide you towards the realisation of your dream.

Don't sit around, waiting to be chosen.

Choose yourself.

## CHAPTER SIX

# WHEN THE GOING GETS TOUGH, KEEP GOING

*"The night is darkest just before the dawn."*

Who was it that said that?

Was it Batman?

I think it might have been Batman.

Well, whoever it was, well done. You nailed it.

The night really is darkest just before the dawn.

The hardest part of any mountain climb is just before you reach the summit. That bit where you've been climbing for so long that your legs are tired and your arms are aching, and you just don't think you can go on any longer – that's the worst part of the climb. But if you just push on a little further, you'll get where you're going, and you'll reach the top, and the view will be beautiful, and it will all be worth it. The trick is just to keep going.

When times are tough, keep going.

When things get hard, keep going.

No matter what, keep going.

It's not that your dream is unattainable. It's not that you dreamed the wrong dream. It's not that you've wandered off the path and ought to turn back. It's just that you need to keep going.

Don't be deterred by difficulty.

Don't be put off by hardship.

If you want it bad enough, then you just have to motor on through whatever lies between where you are now and where you want to be.

All obstacles can be overcome.

There's no mountain that cannot be moved.

The key is not to give up.

Because it's hard to fail when you are determined to succeed.

By the time I was in my early twenties, I was pretty sure I had what it took to become a decent theatre director. After watching Abi direct us all so masterfully on *The Singer* and learning from other directors' mistakes and mishaps, I naively thought that I knew everything there was to know about directing. I thought I'd really nail it when I got my chance.

Turns out, I didn't know what I was talking about.

*Jesus Christ Superstar* had long been one of my favourite musicals since the time I saw it as a kid, and it literally set my whole world on fire, so when Harvest Rain gave me the chance to co-direct the

Andrew Lloyd Webber classic in 2002 with my friend Peter, I was absolutely ecstatic. I must have listened to that original cast recording at least five hundred times as I immersed myself in the score and started dreaming up ideas for what our production could be like. I carried a notebook everywhere I went with me, so I could jot down notes in case I had a flash of inspiration.

For twelve months, I poured my heart and soul into crafting that production; there would be television screens, and multimedia, and metallic scaffolding and leather costumes. We wanted to modernise the show, which at the time I thought was a really original idea but pretty much every production of *Jesus Christ Superstar* since the 1970's has sought to do exactly the same thing! We envisaged Jesus as a rock star, his disciples were his roadies, the Pharisees were his record label, and the ensemble was his adoring fans until they turned on him and killed him, for what reason I couldn't be sure. (Perhaps he released a really dud album? I don't know.) Looking back on it, our premise was not as well thought out as it could have been, and what we ended up with was a bit of a hodge-podge of cool concepts muddled up with some really half-baked ones that either weren't realized very well or didn't really serve the story we were trying to tell or just fell a little flat on delivery. Striking visuals took precedence over clear storytelling, which I have learned is never a recipe for success. Nonetheless, I was proud of the show at the time, but I think what I was most proud of was not so much how it turned out but more the fact that we actually did it. We got up off our butts and did something! Unfortunately, in this industry, you rarely get points for trying – it doesn't matter what you meant or what you intended, it just matters what it is and how it turns out and what it becomes, and looking back at it now I realise that what that show was in the harsh light of day was a well-intended, enthusiastic, passionate misfire. The critics absolutely panned it. One reviewer said, *"The directors are solely responsible for the mess that is Jesus Christ Superstar, and they should never work in this town again."*

Ouch!

I mean, really, ouch!

Never work in this town again? That's the kind of review you get in your worst nightmares, and I got it on the very first major show I ever directed. That certainly wasn't how I pictured things playing out. I always imagined that when I finally did get to direct my first big musical, it would be so stunning and overwhelming and moving and spectacular that people would throw flowers and the season would be extended, and all the reviews would be glowing, and we'd transfer directly to Broadway, and I'd go on immediately to great fame and fortune and international success. I hadn't quite banked on opening the newspaper to read that the show was so bad I should never work again.

But that's the risk you take whenever you put yourself out there. Not everyone is always going to like you or your work. You're not always going to be embraced. You have to find a way to block out all that noise and just power on through. You can't let the setbacks stop you. You learn what you can, and you move onwards. Always onwards.

Thankfully, the bad reviews didn't deter audiences from flocking to see our production in droves. The show may not have been embraced by the critics, but audiences loved it, and by closing night it became clear that the show had been the most financially successful musical that Harvest Rain had ever produced at that time. It also became clear how touch-and-go things were since Harvest Rain had split away from the church, and how desperately the company needed the show to be a hit. In the first few years of operating the company separate from the church, expenses had outweighed the income more often than not, and as a result, there was now a mounting pile of bills that needed to be paid on top of all the regular operating expenses. As we sat in the foyer waiting for the closing night performance to come down, the Parkin brothers confided in me about the company's financial situation.

"We're only just barely making enough money to cover all the bills," Robbie explained.

"But what about all the profit *Superstar* has just made?" I asked.

"Well, it's not really profit," Robbie explained. "It all goes back into paying the rent on the office and insurances and things like that. After all the bills are paid, there's just nothing left."

It was the first time I really got an understanding of how the company worked from a financial perspective. There were show costs (the expenses associated with putting on shows) and then there were operating costs (the expenses associated with running the company from day to day). All of these expenses had to be recouped from ticket sales, so if a show cost $50,000 to produce and managed to sell $70,000 worth of tickets, it may look like it had made $20,000 profit on paper, but really it had just covered its costs and then contributed a little back to the company's overall operating expenses. And then, of course, you had to keep some profit aside to be able to afford to pay the upfront costs on the next show. While *Superstar* itself had made a profit, the money it had made would only just cover operating costs for another three months and would leave nothing aside to mount any new shows. It was becoming clear that it was hard to make money in theatre, at least not the way we were doing it.

"Well, we need to put on another musical and make some more profit," I surmised.

"Musicals are expensive to mount," Robbie explained, "and I don't think we're going to have enough money to get another musical off the ground."

"Well, why don't we put on a play?" I suggested.

"Plays are never as popular as musicals," David said. "They're cheaper, but they bring in less money."

"Well, there must be something we can do to bring in some dollars," I sighed.

I felt terribly frustrated like our hands were tied behind our backs. We needed to produce a musical to make the money we needed to continue operating, but we didn't have the money we needed to mount a musical in the first place. We needed money to make money – it was a vicious cycle.

"I just don't know how much longer we can afford to keep doing this," said Robbie. "We don't want to be just digging a hole for ourselves."

"But we can't just stop!" I said, horrified at the thought.

"We'll just have to keep believing for a miracle!" said Dave, hopefully, but I could tell that both of the brothers were tired and weary from having to keep so many plates spinning in the air as they fought to make the company viable. They'd been working multiple jobs just so they could pay their bills, which left little time after hours to watch over the fledgling company. It had all become too hard and too difficult, and they were running out of steam. Things were looking grim for the future of the company, as the brothers grew weary of the daily fight to keep things afloat.

The next day, I made my way into the office for a 9am start and found myself all alone once again; Robbie was driving his taxi, Dave was off doing freelance design work. It was just me in the office all day, alone with my thoughts, trying to figure out a way forward for the company, trying to work out how to make something out of nothing. I'd accidentally left my lunch at home that morning, so as the day wore on my head began to hurt from all the thinking and the hunger. I snuck a spoonful of sugar from the sugar bowl in the kitchen just to keep me going, but by the end of the day, I was feeling faint and weak from lack of food. As my stomach rumbled, I started thinking about what might become of the company if we couldn't make ends meet, and eventually, my feelings of hunger gave way to feelings of sadness, and anger, and disappointment and bitterness.

I felt defeated.

All the work, all the effort, all the years of volunteering, trying to keep the company afloat - it couldn't all just come to an end. It couldn't all just be for nothing. I hadn't worked for free for three years to see this company just fade away into the night, I thought. I felt so uncertain, and on top of that, I was literally starving. I couldn't see the way forward, so I lay my head down on the desk and cried.

Through my tears, I looked out the window at the park across the street where a giant fig tree stood with huge sprawling branches bearing luscious green leaves. As I watched the leaves blowing gently in the breeze, I thought to myself *"I'm not sure I can do anything to fix the company right this minute, but I can do something to fix my hunger."* In my state of desperation and starvation, I thought to myself, *"I could just go across the road and eat a leaf."*

*"It's technically no different to eating lettuce,"* I thought.

*"I'll just go and nibble on a branch."*

And so I did.

I walked across the street, and I ate a leaf.

I can tell you now that eating a leaf is exactly nothing like eating lettuce.

It was absolutely disgusting, but at least it stopped my hunger pangs and cleared my head. As I stood in that park munching on leaves, I thought about my dream of making a life for myself in the theatre. I thought about the cost of pursuing that dream, how much it was costing the Parkin brothers, and how I was now quite literally starving for my art. And I thought about all the challenges we were facing in keeping Harvest Rain going - all the uncertainty and potential for disaster.

And I realised it was just like eating leaves - we just had to do what had to be done to find a way forward.

Just as I was prepared to eat a handful of leaves to abate my hunger, I would need to be equally prepared to face the tough stuff if that's what was required to keep Harvest Rain afloat. Somehow, somewhere inside of me, I knew I was in the right place, I knew I was doing the right thing, and I knew that if I could just hang on a bit longer, the darkness would be abated by the dawn.

The sun would rise.

I might just have to learn to eat leaves for a while.

I was determined to fight on for the company. The Parkins may have been tired and coming to the end of their tether, and that was understandable, but I wasn't done yet with Harvest Rain, not by a long shot. I got to work, plotting and planning ways that we could turn things around for the company.

To me, I didn't really feel like I had much of a mind for money-making schemes – I wasn't a finance expert, so I didn't really know where to start when it came to figuring out ways to generate more income.

Plus, thinking about money just felt so dull to me.

It felt really cold and dead and joyless.

It felt lonely.

There was no energy in it for me, there was no buzz.

The buzz for me was always in people - in being around like-minded people - in sharing a vision and a common goal. When I thought about that, I felt rich and abundant, not just in a financial sense but in every sense. When I thought of all the creative people that Harvest Rain brought together – when I thought of the family that Harvest Rain had become – I felt empowered and enriched and overflowing with joy. And it suddenly dawned on me that focusing on money was the wrong way to tackle the problem. Money wasn't my forte, and it certainly wasn't my dream. My dream was about people, about gathering like-minded people, about sharing an idea, sharing a passion, sharing a vision and creating community, just like Kermit said at the end of *The Muppet Movie*. I had this flicker of a thought that if I could turn my focus to creating that kind of positive energy by just gathering the people, then the money would follow. Where there is good positive energy, there is abundance, so I figured if I could change the energy, the financial situation could change too.

I remembered the fun I had experienced as a twelve-year-old going along to Saturday drama classes at Harvest Rain. There was such a buzz in those classes. That was good energy. In the years since, Harvest Rain had run a few holidays workshops and one-off masterclasses, but nothing really consistent to engage our young followers. It occurred to me that perhaps gathering like-minded young people for weekly after-school classes and weekend workshops would be a good way to bolster positive energy around the company. Kids have an infectious enthusiasm that permeates everything, and I thought if we could get that kind of energy swirling around us, then only good could come of it.

I didn't even ask the Parkins because I knew they were tired and bogged down by the seeming hopelessness of the situation. I just started planning to mount a school holiday workshop whereby young performers could come and spend a week in the theatre with us rehearsing a show, and at the end of the week, they would perform the show for parents. I knew we had no money to pay for the rights to an existing musical or play, so I decided we would stage an abridged version of Shakespeare's *A Midsummer Night's Dream* (which was well and truly out of copyright), and I started working on an adaption that could easily be performed by teenagers with only five days of rehearsals. I did up a rough budget and worked out that if I ran the workshop myself, the only real cost would be the printing of some flyers to tell everyone about the workshop and the hire of the theatre for a week, and I knew we could cover the cost of that with just a few registrations.

It wouldn't cost us much to muster up a bunch of good energy from passionate young people who loved the theatre as much as we did!

I hacked into Dave's office computer and did up a flyer to promote the holiday workshop. I knew we had an account with our printers, so I could send it off to be printed without up-front payment, which meant the Parkin brothers wouldn't know about the expense for at least a month, by which time I just hoped we'd have received enough registrations to cover the cost of the print!

When the flyers showed up a few days later, I started stuffing and labelling envelopes so we could send them out to everyone on our database, letting them know about our workshop. I didn't realise at the time that Harvest Rain had over ten thousand people on its database, so before long the tiny little office was overflowing with envelopes and labels and flyers, so I called in a few friends to help with the stuffing, and together it took us two weeks to address and fill every envelope. These days, we'd just notify our database via email at the click of a button, but back then (in the dark ages) it really took blood, sweat and tears to make things like that happen! I loaded all the envelopes into my car and transported them down to the post office. We had an account there as well, so I got the whole thing in the mail without spending a cent up front.

And then I waited for the registrations to start rolling in.

I checked the post box every day over that first week, just in case some eager people had a stamp handy to send their registration form back the same day it arrived in their mailbox, but after five days, not a single form had been returned. I went home that weekend feeling a little bit panicked that perhaps I'd made a huge mistake in printing flyers and posting out letters for a workshop that I had never received official approval to run. The bills for the printing and postage were going to come in soon enough, and then the Parkins would find out about my workshop and the expenditure, and I'd be in trouble for going ahead without permission. I had thought we'd get at least five or six registrations which would cover those upfront costs, but after five days of nothing, I spent the weekend preparing for a blasting from the Parkins for squandering the little money that we had without approval.

On Monday morning I walked down to the post box first thing before work, hoping and praying that there would be at least one registration sitting in there that I could process so we could pay those printing bills, and I could avoid the wrath of the Parkins. As I turned the key in the lock, the door on the front of the box burst open from the weight of the wad of envelopes that had been crammed inside. There must have been at least fifty envelopes in there from what I could see, and I had a good feeling that a fair few of them looked like completed registration forms. I literally ran all the way back to the office to open the envelopes, and after all was said and done, seventy-five children had registered to take part in our holiday workshop. We had more than covered the cost of the printing and the postage and the rent of the theatre, and we had gathered an enormous group of young people who would bring with them just the right kind of energy I was hoping for that could blow away the dust and cobwebs of negativity that had begun to form around the company. When Robbie dropped into the office that afternoon in-between taxi shifts, I confessed to him what I had done, and when I held up the wad of completed registration forms in my hand, a broad smile unfolded across his face. I knew I was not about to be chastised. If anything, I think Robbie felt relief that someone else was willing to help carry the load and that the wheels were turning without him having to be the one doing all the pedaling.

By the time the school holidays arrived, we had over one hundred participants enrolled in our workshop, and when they all gathered in the Sydney Street Theatre on the first morning of rehearsals, the energy was absolutely electric. You could literally feel the enthusiasm in the room – the air was thick with their passion and excitement. That week of workshops was absolutely exhausting, putting a show together with a room full of teenagers in just five days. But it was exceedingly joyful at the same time.

The show at the end of the week was a real hoot too.

Our young stars pulled out all the stops to turn in some really impressive performances, and the show played to delighted audiences for five sold-out shows. Just before the final performance, I gathered all one hundred participants in the theatre for a wrap-up discussion and a debrief – they all jokingly called it "Tim-Time", a term that has stuck over the years and is now used any time I give a speech at Harvest Rain – and I invited them all to make suggestions of what sort of training opportunities and experiences they'd like to see us offer in the future. Overwhelmingly, they all wanted to see more holiday workshops, and some even suggested weekly after-school or weekend classes, and from that conversation, the Harvest Rain Talent Academy was born. I knew that where there was passion, then good energy could flow, and Harvest Rain has soared on the wings of that passion ever since.

The money we made from that first-holiday workshop kept the wheels turning for a few more months and bought us time to think about what was next for the company.

"We still don't have enough money in the coffers to put on a musical," Robbie explained at our next meeting.

"Then we should put on a play," I implored.

"We've got a month-long booking coming up at the Sydney Street Theatre. You can put on a play," Robbie instructed, "but you can only spend $10,000 on up front costs. That's all we can afford."

Even back then, $10,000 was not a lot of money to put on a show. Even our tiny cabaret production of *The Randomania Show* had cost $5,000, so bringing the up-front costs of a play in under $10,000 would be a real stretch. But I was prepared to do what needed to be done. I was getting really good at eating leaves.

"If we can sell 3,000 tickets, that will bring in about $75,000, and that should be enough to cover operating costs for another six months," Robbie calculated. "If not….".

His voice trailed off. Nobody ever wanted to say the actual words "we might have to shut down", but you always knew what was being implied. We were definitely nearing the end of the line; the Parkins had spoken. This play had to be low cost for high return, or Harvest Rain would have to close its doors for good.

I grappled in my mind trying to choose a play that would have broad enough appeal to sell 3,000 tickets, or more if we could. With the Sydney Street Theatre booked for a four week engagement, we would have to play to at least half full houses every night if we wanted to meet our target. It didn't seem like an impossible task – after all, *Superstar* had sold out every night for six weeks – but history had proven that plays were never as popular as musicals, so there was no guarantee that we'd meet our ticket sales target.

I realised we needed to choose a play that would feel like a musical, without actually being one. Something that had really broad appeal, was fanciful and whimsical, appealed to families as a whole and didn't seem too high-brow so as to exclude half of our audience. Mostly I thought about all the passionate young actors we had gathered for our holiday workshop and wondered what they'd want to see. What would they convince their friends and family to come along and see with them?

The answer literally hit me in the face one night when the bookshelf above my bed mysteriously collapsed and sent all of the books tumbling down on top of me while I slept. A hardcover book landed right on my head; I grappled in the dark switching on the light only to discover that the book which had just given me a mild concussion was, in fact, my childhood favourite, *The Lion, The Witch and the Wardrobe*. That book to the head was like a lightning bolt of inspiration – this most famous of all the Narnia stories would make a perfect stage play.

The first thing the next morning, I made some inquiries and discovered that a stage-adaption existed, by afternoon I had secured the performance rights, and by the end of the week, auditions were announced, and we were off to the races (or more appropriately, into the wardrobe).

To keep costs to a minimum, I kept the cast as small as possible and ensured that all of the sets were made from existing materials we had in storage, and all of the costumes were created from what we had in stock. The actors wore clothes made out of old curtains we had in the props department, and the set was a conglomeration of old flats and rostra we had lying around. You'd think it would have come out looking a bit cheap and nasty, but with a bit of ingenuity, chewing gum and sticky tape, it turned out looking pretty good. My favourite part of the set was the ornate gold arch we built all around the outskirts of the proscenium; the script called for a Narrator, and I had decided that I would cast multiple people in the Narrator role, and have them play statues who would live up in this proscenium arch, frozen still while the audience entered the theatre. Then, as the house lights dimmed, they would spring to life and climb down on to the stage and walk the audience through the play, before climbing back into position at the close of the show. It was a very satisfying kind of "book-end" idea to start and finish the play, realised beautifully with our proscenium arch made out of second-hand timber, old pipes, bed sheets and some gold paint. It was extremely effective, and cost us next to nothing to pull off!

It was a busy time, rehearsing the show by night, and working in the office taking bookings all day. From the moment we put the show on sale, the phones rang off the hook with people wanting tickets, which was a really good sign we might meet our ticket sales target by closing night, but it meant I was completely run off my feet. I had no time to do anything else but answer those phones all day and rehearse the show by night. Things ran very smoothly as we put the show together, and after the messy way in which I realised my vision for *Superstar*, I was determined that I wouldn't lose control of the reigns on this one. I would pay attention to what it was actually becoming, not just to how good the original idea might have been, and by doing that the show began to flourish into something quite special. I was also determined to give myself plenty of time to watch the show running from start to finish prior to it opening so I could properly critique and finesse the work before an audience saw it, and also to give the actors playing the statues plenty of opportunity to practice sitting motionless in the proscenium arch for half an hour before the show each night! So we started doing full runs more than two weeks out from the first performance. I forced myself to watch the runs objectively as if I was an audience member seeing it for the first time. After all, that really is the director's job – to speak on behalf of the audience and inform the actors how their performances are being received. A director is the actor's eyes and ears in the audience, and I took that role seriously. I was really pleased with the show once I saw it all run together – it felt snappy and energetic, and the story unfolded just as I had hoped. It was magical and charming, and the cast had wonderful chemistry and camaraderie that seemed to permeate through the entire show. I had a hunch that this one might be well received, and that hunch proved to be correct.

On opening night, the show played beautifully, flawlessly, perfectly, with great precision and timing, good energy and flow. At the end of the performance, as the statues moved back up into their places in the proscenium, the audience began applauding as they climbed, and by the time the statues were back in place, the audience were on their feet, cheering and whistling and hollering and hooting. There was an immense sense of joy amongst the patrons as they left the theatre, and an elderly couple accosted me on their way out of the foyer, saying with tears in their eyes that the show had reminded them of their childhood and had made them feel young again. It all felt very special, indeed.

The next day in the office was busier than any other day I had ever experienced at Harvest Rain before. From the moment I set foot in the office, the phones rang off the hook with people demanding tickets to see the show, and as the day wore on, we had to start a waiting list because performances were selling out left, right and centre. There simply wasn't enough tickets to meet demand and by the start of the following week, the entire season had completely sold out. We had sold 6,000 tickets in total – twice as many as we had hoped to sell - and to meet the demand we had to add an extra week of shows to the season. Once those extra performances sold out, our total sales tally sat at well over 7,000 tickets sold - over $150,000 in sales - by far the highest grossing show Harvest Rain had ever produced to date. The profit the show made was more than enough to clear the mounting pile of bills and contribute to operating costs for many months ahead.

In the end, *The Lion, The Witch and the Wardrobe* really did save the day. On the eve of the final performance, we took a photo on the stage with each of the actors holding up a giant card with a number on it, that when viewed in sequence read "$150,000". I'm not sure any of the actors really understood the significance of that moment, but for the Parkin brothers, and for me it was huge.

It was a miracle.

It was a gift.

We had found a way to move forward.

After the show closed, the Parkins jointly agreed that I should take on the role of Artistic Director of Harvest Rain, since I had been unofficially operating in that role for well over a year, and they agreed that it was time for me to be paid for the work that I was doing. My three years of volunteering had come to an end – there would be no more need for eating leaves, at least not in the literal sense. There would be plenty more hurdles to overcome and challenges to face and tough times to push through, but at that moment, I was living the dream. At the age of twenty-two, I was the Artistic Director of

Harvest Rain, doing exactly what I had always desired.

If there's one thing I have learned from all the years of slogging it out in theatre, it's that when the going gets tough, you have to keep going. You have to find a way to push through. It's all too easy to see a roadblock and turn back or look for an easier path. But sometimes, the rocky, treacherous path is the only way to get where you're going. It's not always going to be smooth sailing. You have to learn to navigate the rough seas. And once the storm has passed, there will always be a rainbow. Just hang on – it's coming. The clouds will part soon, and you will see it if you can just find a way to keep going.

Life is like a video game, where each level of the game prepares you for the rigour of the next one. You have to master the first level before you're ready to level up to the second, and on the second level you will find a whole new range of challenges that will grow you and prepare you for the demands of the third, and so on and so on. Life wants to level you up, and you have to let it.

Don't avoid the challenge. Don't run from the roadblock. Don't balk when the only thing left to eat is a handful of leaves.

You just grab on to that branch and start munching, and you do what needs to be done to get up to that next level. Because in the end, it's very hard to fail when you're determined to succeed.

## CHAPTER SEVEN
# WHO DO YOU THINK YOU ARE?

If you've ever chased a dream, you've probably met Doubt before.

Doubt lives right outside your door – right outside that quiet place where you can dream without boundaries or ridicule or persecution – and as soon as you set out on your journey to follow your dream, Doubt will almost always try to come along for the ride.

Doubt will say:

*"You don't know what you're doing.*

*You're not strong enough or brave enough to make it to the end of this road.*

*You're not good enough to succeed.*

*Best turn back now."*

And you might be brave enough to run on ahead a little, to get a bit of distance on the road, but you'll soon find out that Doubt can run just as fast as you can, and it has a vexing little question to ask you that will stop you in your tracks unless you can provide a decent answer:

*"Who do you think you are?"*

That's what Doubt will scream as it runs down the road after you.

That's what you'll hear as you try to outrun your fears.

*"Who do you think you are?"*

Whatever you do, make sure you have a good answer.

Because whatever you say, Doubt is going to agree.

If your answer is confidently and unabashedly "I am a winner," then Doubt will agree and start to fall back and submit under the strength and clarity of the notion of your own abilities.

But if deep down you think that you are unworthy, or unlucky, or not good enough, or not smart enough, or not brave enough, or not old enough or just simply not enough, then Doubt is going to agree with that too, and start to feed off the strength of your lack of belief, and grow, and grow, and grow until that core belief severely limits what might be possible for you.

Most often, we do not believe things because they are true; things become true because we believe them. So your answer to the question of "Who do you think you are" might just be the most important answer you ever give, because that answer will set your course, and either help you immeasurably or hinder you entirely as you journey on the path towards the realisation of your dreams.

I first made friends with Doubt at the age of twenty-two, when I found myself living the life I had always dreamed of at the helm of a growing arts organization, mastering the art of producing pro-am productions in a little 300-seat theatre in Brisbane with limited funds, no real clout and no real idea what I was doing. I was producing and directing a whole range of different musicals – from *The Wiz* to *Little Shop of Horrors*, *Into the Woods* to Disney's *Beauty and the Beast* - each one helping to solidify Harvest Rain's growing reputation as a respected provider of musical theatre entertainment. But for all the success we were enjoying, I still didn't really know the first thing about running a company, and most of the time I felt like a total imposter. I was not university trained. I didn't have many friends or connections in the world of theatre. I felt very much on the outskirts of the industry, as if other established producers and theatre-makers were looking down on me with a kind of disdain, like I was some sort of intruder who had broken in through the back door of the industry and I didn't really deserve to be there. And the truth was, I HAD broken in through the back door of the industry, so maybe I didn't really deserve to be there! I was just making it up as I went along. Of course, I now realise that EVERYONE is making it up as they go along, but at the time I felt like I was the only one! For the first time in my life, I encountered Doubt – overwhelming Doubt – and when Doubt asked me the question "Who do you think you are?" my response was, "I am just a little guy. I am not experienced enough or old enough to be taken seriously. Maybe this is as far as I will go."

And Doubt agreed and began to grow.

Since taking the helm of Harvest Rain, I had started

daydreaming about how we might be able to open the organisation up to school leavers who wanted to experience what it was like to be part of the day to day operations of a working theatre company. In my head, I imagined we could offer a full-time musical theatre training course that was something akin to an internship, where participants could spend a year coming in to Harvest Rain each day and learning on the job, working behind the scenes helping to put our shows together, performing on stage, working backstage and generally honing their craft as part of a working theatre company. In my mind, it would basically be a way of formalising the kind of on-the-job training I had received volunteering at Harvest Rain for all those years when I started out. Every time I pondered the idea of running some kind of full-time course, I felt a bubble of excitement rise up inside me, but it would soon be swallowed up by a rush of uncertainty.

Doubt would always rise.

It would say to me "Who do you think you are?" and I could never find a good answer.

I didn't know if anyone would take me seriously as a mentor to emerging performers, especially since I was still so young and finding my own way. I started to second-guess myself and give in to feelings of inadequacy. I felt small and insignificant like I would be laughed at by everyone if I stood up and said that I wanted to start a program where young artists could learn about the theatre under my guidance.

So I put the idea aside.

I pushed it away.

I didn't feel worthy enough to follow where that dream would lead.

Despite my own feelings of doubt and unworthiness, business really was booming, which meant we were able to employ a few new staff members in the office to help me run the company daily. One of the first people I employed was Callum Mansfield. Since meeting Callum on Harvest Rain's production of *Oliver!*, the two of us had become thick as thieves. We were the best of friends, and our friendship in life began to blossom into a great working relationship as well. Callum had always been a great dancer, but in his teens he developed a passion for choreography which really complemented my passion for directing and producing, so it made sense to find a way to bring him into the Harvest Rain fold in an official capacity so the company could benefit from his burgeoning choreographic skills. Of course, working at Harvest Rain always meant wearing many hats, so while Callum may have been choreographing shows for us by night, he would be answering phones at the front desk by day, just like I had for so many years. Callum's presence in the office gave me time to just focus on growing the company and "lay the tracks in front of the train", so to speak. The company was growing too big for me to run the race alone, so it was incredibly encouraging to have like-minded, passionate helpers around me who could help me reach the finish line.

One morning, the office phone rang.

The office was still not much larger than a standard bedroom, so Callum was sitting just across the room from me when he answered the call. After a few pleasantries, he put his hand over the mouthpiece and whispered across to me, "Marina Prior's manager is on the phone for you".

I laughed out loud.

Marina Prior was Australia's most prominent, most successful leading lady in musical theatre. She'd played Christine in *The Phantom of the Opera*. She'd been in *Cats* and *Les Miserables*. She'd recorded albums and been on television. She was famous – proper famous. A household name. Why on earth would Marina Prior's manager be calling me? It had to be a joke.

"Hang up," I said. "It's a prank call".

Callum dutifully hung up the phone.

"I think that was for real," he said. "He says Marina wants to meet you at the gala tonight".

Harvest Rain had been asked to provide an opening number for a fundraiser dinner in the city that evening for which Marina was the headline act. We had rallied a bunch of our youth theatre kids, and

Callum had choreographed a big song and dance number to kick off the night - I had thought there was a chance Marina might see our work at the gala, but I never envisaged that she would want to meet me in person.

It had to be a hoax, I thought.

I put it out of my mind.

That night when I arrived at the fundraiser dinner, I bumped into my friend Duncan who was the organiser of the event.

"Marina Prior was asking after you at sound check," he said. "Do you know her?"

"No," I said with a lump of nervousness in my throat. "Never met her."

"Well, she seems to know you," Duncan said with a smile. "She really wants to catch up with you tonight."

I felt all the blood drain out of my head and rush down into my feet. I felt like I was being summoned to the principal's office (only the principal was Australia's leading lady of musical theatre). At the time, I had a fairly poor track record when it came to meeting famous people. I'd once lined up for hours to meet Sophie Monk in the Queen Street Mall and nearly vomited on her with nerves and excitement when she signed my poster and said I was cute. I'd had a similar encounter with Bert Newton at a theatre stage door years earlier, and then there was this other time when I briefly worked at a call centre, and I somehow ended taking a call from Tom Cruise and I sort of screamed down the line at him, "Show me the money!" and then giggled like an idiot and accidentally hung up on him. (That's a whole other story – tell you some other time). I just got really stupid around famous people, and so naturally when I knew for sure that Marina Prior wanted to meet me, I did the only sensible thing I could think of.

I hid.

I spent most of the evening sliding down in my chair and hiding behind my menu. I didn't think I was significant or important enough to warrant the attention of someone of Marina's calibre, and that limiting belief stopped me from being able to accept the notion that someone like Marina Prior would ever want to seek me out.

I was nobody special.

Why should someone like her want to meet someone like me?

Right at the end of the night, I felt a tap on my shoulder. I turned around and there she was, standing right beside me.

"Hello, I'm Marina", she said, as if I didn't know.

I said something stupid. I can't even remember what. I was just trying not to pass out. Somehow my lips moved, and sounds came out, and we ended up chatting for quite a little while and eventually Marina told me that she was working with a bunch of actors down in Melbourne and they were looking to start a small theatre company, and she wanted to get my advice on how to go about it all.

Just to recap: One of the most famous and successful figures in the history of musical theatre in Australia wanted my advice on how to start a theatre company.

WHAT IN THE WORLD WAS GOING ON?

Surely she had Andrew Lloyd Webber on speed dial.

No doubt she could have called Cameron Mackintosh for assistance.

But no, she wanted MY advice.

I have no idea how I didn't just wet my pants right there and then.

Over the coming weeks, we emailed back and forth, and Marina made plans for me to fly down to Melbourne to work with her troupe. I'd hardly travelled anywhere before, so the plane trip was exciting all by itself, but once I got to Melbourne, Marina welcomed me into her home like an old friend and took me into rehearsals with her theatre troupe to critique their work as if I was Stanislavski. She seemed to hang off my every word. When I spoke, she listened attentively and said things like "That's really profound" and "You've got such a good eye for this sort of thing". I didn't feel profound at all - I was mostly just focusing on not melting into a puddle on the floor. I was an absolute nobody who had only directed a handful of low budget shows in a tiny little theatre in Brisbane, but for some reason, Marina treated me like I knew what I was talking about and like I was on her level. I kept expecting her to suddenly realise that she'd made a mistake and brought the wrong person to Melbourne, but it never happened. She seemed to respect me, though I couldn't figure out why, and slowly, because Marina seemed to believe in me, I started to believe in me too. As the days wore on, whenever I felt like I wasn't worthy of being there, I would think to myself, "Well, Marina Prior thinks you're good. You must be doing something right," and it would make me stand a little taller and hold my head a little higher. Marina's faith in me felt like a permission slip allowing me to have faith in myself, and slowly, my answer to the question "Who do you think you are?" started to change.

"What's next for Harvest Rain?" Marina asked as I left for the airport at the end of our time together in Melbourne. Had she asked me a week or two earlier, I would have stumbled over a sheepish answer and said something about just producing more shows and keeping the wheels in motion, but with my new-found confidence and sense of self-belief, I felt emboldened to proudly back myself and the bigness of my dreams.

"I'd like to start a full-time musical theatre course," I said, saying out loud for the first time the idea that had been brewing in my mind since I'd scribbled it down in my diary when I was seventeen.

"What an excellent idea," Marina said enthusiastically, without even blinking. She didn't seem to think the idea was silly, or that I was too young to be doing that, or that it wouldn't work out. She thought it was an excellent idea, and as I flew home that afternoon, I felt completely empowered by her unequivocal endorsement of my dream. During the flight, I started earnestly hatching a plan detailing how we might be able to start this full-time course as soon as the following year, frantically scribbling down notes on the back of my plane ticket. By the time the plane touched down in Brisbane, I was completely determined – this was a happening thing, and it didn't take long for me to gather the small staff at Harvest Rain to start brainstorming the kind of program we might be able to offer. After a long period of deliberation, we decided that we should gently float the idea of a full-time course with our youth theatre students, both past and present, just to gauge whether there was any real interest in the program. We thought that perhaps we would end up with five or six people who might want to be part of this training program in the new year, but within a month of quietly announcing it, we had received over 150 expressions of interest in the course! We knew then that we were really on to something, and so we began making our plans in earnest to commence a full-time course the very next year, emboldened by Marina's belief in my vision.

Doubt quickly took the wind out of my sails though, when the church who owned the Sydney Street Theatre informed us that they would not be renewing our lease in the new year and, as such, the theatre would no longer be available for us to use as a performance space, or as a home for our newly planned full-time musical theatre course. After twenty-two years performing at the Sydney Street Theatre, Harvest Rain would be without a home.

The news was completely devastating. The Sydney Street Theatre was more than just a theatre to me and to so many people who felt like part of the Harvest Rain family.

It was like home.

It was a place to belong.

It was where we had grown up.

It was where our love of theatre had been ignited.

The thought of no longer being able to perform there after more than two decades was sickening, an absolute kick to the guts.

And then, it was terrifying.

Where would we go?

Where would we produce our shows?

Would our audiences follow us?

Where would they even follow us too?

And worst of all, we'd just decided to start this full-time musical theatre course in the promise that our students would be involved in the day to day running of a working theatre company, and that theatre company suddenly had no home, nowhere to perform and nowhere to exist.

It felt like we were a plant being uprooted and discarded, a fish being plucked from the sea and left to die on the land.

Suddenly the staff were all looking to me.

The board were looking to me.

Actors, directors, creative people who had worked with us for years and who all loved Harvest Rain and cared about its future and their place in it, were all looking to me and wondering what was next.

And I was wondering the same thing.

I just didn't have the answer.

And I felt very small and very alone, and very scared.

And then Doubt came to me again with that same question it had asked me so many times before.

"Who do you think you are?"

I felt battered and weary, and the best responses I could muster felt like questions in themselves.

"I am brave?"

"I am a winner?"

"I am going to do great things?"

In a moment of major self-doubt, I reached out to Marina for guidance. I'd felt so emboldened by her belief in me when we first met, I thought that now she might be able to jumpstart my confidence once again with a shot of her infectious enthusiasm. I regaled her with my stories and cried about how beaten down I felt and about how I just couldn't see anything on the road ahead, only darkness and uncertainty. When I'd finally finished my sob story, she took me by the arms, looked me in the eyes and said, "Take a day off and go climb a mountain or sit on a rock somewhere and get still, and don't get up until you get clarity! It's only in the silence that you will ever be able to find your answer."

Clarity was what I needed; that, or a million dollars and a new theatre. I trusted my friend Marina enough to know that I should probably do what she said, so I took a day off and drove up into the mountains. I parked my car and walked into the bush for about an hour until I came to a clearing and saw a giant boulder on the edge of a cliff looking out over the valley and down all the way to the ocean. I perched myself on its peak and sat there for a few minutes taking in the view – I was so high up, and the vista was so vast that I felt like I was looking out over the whole world. It was so peaceful and quiet, I could hear only the sound of a few birds singing and the wind rustling the leaves of the trees.

And then I heard the voice of Doubt whisper to me gently:

*"Who do you think you are?"*

I didn't have an answer, and it wasn't really the question I was interested in, so I moved to a different rock, as if somehow on a different rock the Doubt might go away or say something different. But, Doubt really only ever says one thing, and after a few moments sitting on my new rock, it whispered again:

*"Who do you think you are?"*

I didn't care about that question.

That had nothing to do with anything, I thought, and I moved again to another rock.

This time I chose one perched right on the edge of the cliff, jutting right out from all the others, overlooking the valley below and all the way out to the sea. Sitting there on that rock, I felt afraid. I couldn't stop thinking about going back down the mountain and back to life and back to trying to figure out a way forward for Harvest Rain without the Sydney Street Theatre, and the fear crept up my spine and wrapped its icy hand tightly around my mind.

I needed answers.

I needed clarity.

But all I could find was Doubt.

It asked me once again:

*"Who do you think you are?"*

Anger bubbled up inside me; I wanted to explode with intense rage. I was tired of Doubt's questions and didn't want to give an answer. But Doubt kept pressing, and the more it pressed, the angrier I became. I wanted to scream at Doubt for trying to hold me back. I wanted to rant and rave against the uncertainty.

How dare this Doubt show up on this rock to try and hold me back, I thought to myself.

How dare it try to stop me from finding peace and clarity by asking that stupid question over and over again.

I wanted to smack it in the head.

I wanted to throw it right off that cliff.

How dare it!

How very dare it, I kept thinking in my mind as I seethed at the presence of Doubt.

And then suddenly, the rage overwhelmed me and consumed me, and I leapt to my feet and stood on that rock and screamed into the sunlight:

*"I am brave.*

*I am strong.*

*I am resilient.*

*I am fearless.*

*I am big.*

*I am fierce.*

*I am determined.*

*I am a winner.*

*And I am not leaving here until I get some clarity!"*

My voice echoed down into the valley below me.

I scared the living daylights out of a lizard that was sunning itself on a nearby rock, and I think I scared myself too.

What just came out of my mouth?

What was that verbal explosion?

After spending the past few months worrying that I wasn't good enough to be doing what I was doing, and certainly not good enough to do anything more, the feeling of vociferously, aggressively, unabashedly declaring my own awesomeness out loud felt utterly incredible.

I felt a hundred feet tall.

I felt invincible.

I felt worthy.

And I felt the stillness and solitude on that mountaintop rush over me and wrap itself around me.

And then I felt completely at peace.

I sat in tranquil silence for another few hours, just listening, getting peaceful with myself, tuning in to the tranquility that seemed to be enveloping me. Something about being surrounded by the serenity of nature, away from the hustle and bustle and the noise of the city, helped me to align with a sense of stillness - a sense of myself - that I hadn't really known before. The voice of Doubt had always been so loud, but here in the stillness I could hear a new gentle voice, almost like a whisper, and it seemed to be answering Doubt's questions for me. It seemed to know who I was, and it seemed to think I was pretty splendid, and it seemed to want me to know that too. Perhaps the whisper had always been there, quietly encouraging me onwards, but the noise of my life had prevented me from tuning into it. Now in the stillness, this gentle voice - this gentle knowing — brought me a sense of peace and clarity that I'd not experienced before, and even though it didn't directly provide me with the answer to my problems, I felt overcome with the knowledge and the certainty that all was well. That I shouldn't be worried. That I was worthy. That if I just walked forward in this sense of calm and clarity that all the pieces would fall in to place and everything would turn out fine.

The next morning, when I got to work, there was an envelope on my desk with the QPAC logo emblazoned in the corner. I thought it was a marketing letter promoting upcoming shows at the Arts Centre, but when I opened it I saw that it was a letter from the CEO of QPAC, addressed personally to me. In the letter, he outlined how impressed he was with the quality of the work Harvest Rain was producing and wanted to formally invite us to become one of QPAC's resident companies by presenting regular productions in the 800-seat Playhouse at the Centre.

We would not be homeless, after all.

And we'd be upsizing!

Not long after, an email arrived from the landlord of an unused warehouse on the north side of Brisbane, saying that if we ever needed extra space for rehearsals or workshops we should consider taking up a lease.

And just like that, we found a home for our new full-time course and the Brisbane Academy of Musical Theatre was born.

Screaming my response to Doubt's question from the top of that mountain not only brought me great clarity and peace but also a connection to my true inner self that seemed to unlock a sense of flow that brought an answer to every problem I was currently facing. In an instant, it seemed, my fortunes had changed. There was suddenly a way forward where previously I could see none. By changing my mindset, by affirming myself and by aligning with the peace and well-being that was the essence of my true inner being, I changed the nature of what life was bringing to me.

Life responded to my self-certainty.

My belief became my truth.

I have learned that when Doubt asks you "Who do you think you are?", it's not asking as a means of stopping you or slowing you down. It's not asking because it wants you to hang your head in shame and declare that you're nothing and nobody. It's asking to give you an opportunity to declare support for yourself. It's asking so that you will give the whole of your being an instruction as to how you wish to operate. It's asking to trigger a response in you that will force you to align with the truth of who you really are.

There is no more important question than "Who do you think you are", and likewise there is no more important answer. What you say in response will define the way your life unfolds, because what you believe becomes your truth.

You can only win if you know you are a winner.

You will only succeed if you believe you are a success.

Mindset is everything.

Perhaps you need to climb a mountain and sit on a rock to seek your own answers to the question.

Perhaps you already know the answer, but you're afraid to say it out loud.

Perhaps, you dislike the question because you have not yet found the courage to align with your true self and declare your own support for yourself, and you'd rather stick your head in the sand and try a different question.

But that is the only question that really matters.

It's the only question that really counts.

And your answer should be nothing less than:

*"I am an exquisite human being capable of doing whatever I put my mind to. I am strong, I am brave, I am not afraid, and I am going to get where I'm going, just watch me go."*

Sometimes it is hard to look past our flaws and shortcomings and see our own potential. I think it is human nature to identify our weaknesses before we celebrate our strengths. But we must learn to become our own champions, our own cheer squad, and we must give ourselves permission to believe that success is possible if we ever actually hope to succeed.

What you think and believe about yourself matters because what you believe you eventually become.

So, tell me…

Who do you think you are

## CHAPTER EIGHT
# NEVER MIND THE CRABS

I've never been into fishing.

Never thought the idea of standing on the water's edge clutching a fishing rod for hours on end seemed terribly interesting.

Perhaps that's why my Grandmother took me crab hunting instead.

I was ten years old, and my younger sister and I were staying with our two cousins at our Grandparents' house for the school holidays. Biddy – that's what we called my Grandmother, don't ask me why – thought that taking us down to the creek to hunt for crabs and yabbies would be a fun way to pass the time. Sounded as dull as fishing to me, but nevertheless, off we trudged down to the creek, Biddy clutching a make-shift crab pot and a fishing rod and the four of us with buckets in hand ready to catch some mud crabs.

When we reached the banks of the local creek, Biddy placed the crab pot in the water and encouraged each of us to put our buckets down on the nearby rocks. Then Biddy sat us down on the grass by the creek, and we waited. In hindsight, I'm not sure if Biddy ever intended for us to catch any crabs or whether she had just come up with an ingenious way to keep us occupied all afternoon waiting for crabs to get caught in the pot. Either way, we sat there for a good long while, eyes glued to the pot, waiting for any sign of a crab or a yabbie. But none came.

"How many crabs do you think we will catch, Bid?" I asked after half an hour had passed.

"Maybe two or three, if we're lucky," she replied.

"Then why did we bring so many buckets?" I asked. "Two or three could all fit in the same one."

"Oh, you can't do that," she said, sounding incensed. "It's cruel to put them all in the one bucket."

Catching, killing and eating crabs was fine, but putting them all in the one bucket was cruel? That made no sense to me, and I told her so.

"If you take three or four crabs and put them in the one bucket together, they'll all try to kill each other," she explained, "so you have to keep them separate."

I may have only been ten years old, but I could see some flaws in that logic. Didn't she want the crabs to die anyway? Why would it be a problem if they killed each other? It would save her the trouble later. Besides, it sounded like a made-up story to me. Why would crabs try and kill each other if they were kept in the same bucket?

Our trip to the creek that day proved fruitless, and by sunset, we traipsed back home to tell Pop all about our adventures. When I jovially told my grandfather about Biddy's reasoning behind bringing so many buckets to the creek with us, he shook his head with a smile.

"Biddy just doesn't like to see them fight," he said. "Mud crabs can be tricky. If you put a mud crab in a bucket by itself it will just climb right out, so you have to put it in a bucket with other mud crabs. When they're all together, if one of the crabs tries to climb out, the other crabs gang up on it and pull it down. I saw it one time where this persistent little crab kept trying to climb out of the bucket, so the other crabs just pulled it down and broke its arms. Killed it. It's just how crabs are."

Crabs are weird, I thought and resolved to never go crab hunting again.

Turns out, though, that it's not just crabs that behave that way.

Humans do it too.

At the start of my journey when I was dreaming of the way things would be once I had reached all of my goals, I never gave much thought to how other people would respond to my dream, other than to just assume that everyone would be thrilled and proud of me.

Turns out that wasn't always the case.

Not everybody can handle the altitude where you're climbing to, and rather than proudly watch you go off in pursuit of the summit, there's plenty of people in life who would rather keep you on their level, keep you small, keep you in that safe, non-threatening space somewhere halfway up the mountain where they are, where the summit will always be out of your reach, just like they feel it is out of theirs.

They'll try to pull you back down into the bucket with them.

That is the way of the crabs.

As we made the move from presenting shows at Sydney Street to producing out of the Queensland Performing Arts Complex, we felt the full wrath of crab mentality for the first time. I expected people would be really pleased for us, that after two decades slogging it out in a small venue, Harvest Rain was spreading its wings and taking its well-earned place in one of Australia's premier entertainment venues. I thought that everyone would clap and cheer for us, but that didn't turn out to be the case.

We staged a huge production of *Joseph and the Amazing Technicolor Dreamcoat* at QPAC (I missed the chance to play Joseph all those years ago, but eventually I got to produce him) and the show featured a massive chorus made up of our many youth theatre students, as well as a sizeable group of local amateur and pro-am musical theatre performers. It was a really wonderful marriage of up and coming performers working alongside more seasoned actors, which was what Harvest Rain was all about. Audiences loved the show - thank goodness they followed us from Sydney Street and brought their friends - but a quick trawl through the comments in my Facebook feed made it clear that some people in the industry were less than impressed by what we were doing and the strides we were taking, and they weren't afraid to be vocal about it, sharing their feelings all over their social media platforms. These people thought that there was no place for amateur or pro-am theatre at QPAC – they assumed that Harvest Rain was making a fortune on ticket sales and therefore they should be sharing it with the actors. Nothing could have been further from the truth. The larger seating capacity in the Playhouse gave us the ability to sell more tickets and bring in more money, it's true, but it also increased our costs exponentially, and on most of our shows we were barely breaking even. It was a challenge every day to make ends meet.

The intense criticism really hit me hard, especially because a good deal of it was directed at me personally as the head of Harvest Rain. I started to feel like one of those crabs in my grandmother's bucket having its arms broken for trying to climb out to freedom.

I didn't want to be ridiculed. I wanted to be liked.

I didn't want to be made fun of. I wanted to be encouraged.

I didn't want people to hate me. I wanted people to be proud of me.

But no matter what we did, this small group of noisy voices on the internet were always ready to throw stones, so I started trying to appease them.

In 2012, we announced a production of the musical *Hairspray* at QPAC, and for this one, I made sure that while the ensemble would still be made up of our full-time students and local amateurs, all of the principal cast were paid professionally, just so that the nay-sayers would have less ammunition for their negative critique.

That'll impress those crabs, I thought.

They'll have to love us now.

But in my eagerness to assuage their crabby-criticisms, I made a mistake that ended up giving the crabs something else to target, and this time it literally blew up the internet.

I opened the Courier Mail a few weeks out from opening night to see our leading lady's photograph splashed across the header on the front page with the caption "HARVEST RAIN CAUGHT OUT" emblazoned above it. Acting on a tip-off from one of the local crabs, the paper was alleging that we had photo-shopped our lead actress' head on to the body of the performer who had played Tracy Turnblad on Broadway and used that composite image for all of our marketing material. The truth was that, in our haste to prepare marketing material well before our costumes had been completed, we had used the skirt and blouse from an existing stock image to enhance the photograph of our own Tracy Turnblad. The story in the paper made it sound like we had committed something akin to high treason or genocide, and the minute it hit the stands, the story just exploded across the internet. Our phones rang off the hook with other news outlets seeking comment from us, and Facebook went insane with people raking us over the coals. In hindsight, it was a misstep and a great lesson for us all, and I wish we hadn't embellished the photograph just so we could have avoided all the fuss that ensued!

In the afternoon of the day that the story blew up, I received an invitation to do an in-studio interview the following morning on ABC breakfast radio. It was the highest rating radio program at the time, so I felt like it was the best place to set the record straight, but what it turned out to be was a total ambush. The announcer was lovely to me off-air, but the minute we got on the air, he hit me hard with a barrage of rapid-fire questions about the photo-shop scandal, and it quickly degenerated into an interrogation, which I just wasn't prepared for.

I was left fumbling and looking foolish, live on air.

Then, out of nowhere, he started confronting me with a whole new set of accusations about not paying our actors and taking advantage of performers, and somewhere in the middle of it all I just kind of went numb and sort of zoned out. It felt like the world was caving in on me. As I left the studio, stunned and in shock, the host leaned across the desk and said to me, "Well, you got ten minutes at the top of the 7 o'clock hour. Primetime. You can't complain about that."

Maybe he was right.

No publicity is bad publicity.

Ticket sales went through the roof straight after the interview, so clearly the listeners hadn't been deterred by my on-air slaughtering, but I felt completely shattered. I desperately wanted to please everyone, and I wanted everyone to like me. Being vilified and attacked in the press was mortally wounding. I felt ashamed and embarrassed and terribly alone.

"I just want to run the kind of company that everyone can get behind and support," I thought to myself. "Maybe if we could afford to pay all of our actors, then everyone would get off our backs and start liking us again."

Borne out of my intense desire to silence the haters, I started hatching a plan to evolve Harvest Rain from a pro-am company that gave emerging artists the opportunity to work alongside seasoned professionals, into a company focused soley on providing professional employment to working actors. I was so desperate to be liked by the people who were throwing stones at us that I forgot about the thousands of audience members who loved our shows, and the hundreds of young people and their parents who loved our youth theatre classes and the full-time musical theatre course we were now running. All I could think about was converting the haters into lovers.

Dammit, they had to love us!

They just had to!

So, in 2013, we secured the rights to the classic musical *Oklahoma!*, booked a week in the QPAC Concert Hall and began preparing to stage our very first fully professional production. There was a lot to learn working in the new format with payment of actors and creatives to consider. When you're working on an amateur or pro-am show, it's easy to involve a large number of people in a production because there's no payroll to consider; you can have an ensemble with twenty people, or thirty, or forty, or however many you would like, and it doesn't really affect the budget. Working professionally, however, means each person has to be paid, so you can only have as many people in your show as your budget will allow. This was one of the first challenges we encountered - our regular performers were so used to us making room for very large ensembles, but when we finished auditions for *Oklahoma!* and our cast of 17 performers was announced, many of our regulars felt terribly displaced. Previously, our full-time students at the Brisbane Academy of Musical Theatre were always involved in the show as well, but because it was a professional production, they couldn't take part, and nor could our youth theatre students, much to their chagrin and disappointment.

The show itself turned out to be a marvellous production, and it was a wonderful achievement to be able to provide employment for musical theatre actors in Queensland, but the abrupt change to the way we did things ended up displacing an awful lot of the people who had loved and supported us for a very long time.

So now the lovers hated us, and the haters hated us.

I just couldn't win!

Not long after *Oklahoma!* closed, Broadway star Kristin Chenoweth announced that she would be touring Australia in the winter of 2013, and I hatched this crazy idea that I might be able to convince her to come to visit our new studios and sit down with me for a Q&A with our students and conduct a master-class. I thought it would be a great way to ingratiate ourselves with our long-time supporters who had started to feel sidelined in the professional transition, giving them the chance to learn from one of the greatest living musical theatre performers on the planet. I also thought it might give us some clout by association, which might give the crabs some pause for thought so they could stop throwing their stones. Aside from her extensive work on television shows like *The West Wing, Glee* and *Pushing Daisies*, Kristin had also appeared in a bunch of films and recorded plenty of best-selling albums, and she held a special place in the hearts of musical theatre lovers across the globe for originating the role of Glinda in the Broadway smash-hit musical,

*Wicked*. Kristin was a bona fide international celebrity, so when I sent an email off to her management inviting her to visit us in Brisbane for an interview, I didn't really expect to ever hear back. You can imagine my surprise when, the very next day, her manager called me and said Kristin would love to sit down with me, do an interview and hold a masterclass at our new studios.

What a coup!

"Take that crabs!" I thought to myself with a smile.

We decided that the interview should be filmed so that anyone who couldn't attend the workshop would still be able to experience the event online, so I spent weeks researching Kristin's life to make sure that I had some intelligent questions to ask her when the cameras finally rolled. By the day of the interview, I felt like I knew her life story even better than she did. Kristin arrived quite early, moving slowly and deliberately as she was recovering from a severe neck injury she had sustained a year earlier on the set of *The Good Wife*.

"I'm on painkillers," she said, as she gingerly sat down on the couch in my office. "Don't think I'm rude if I keep looking at the wall, it's just I can't turn my neck."

We had over an hour to kill before the interview was due to start, and while the rest of the staff were busy preparing the venue and corralling the masterclass participants into the theatre, Kristin and I got to sit and chat in the quiet of my office. It was pretty surreal seeing someone so famous sitting on my couch, but then at the same time, it felt completely normal. Kristin was kind and disarmingly friendly, and after twenty minutes of chatting, I felt like I'd known her my whole life.

"So, tell me Tim," she said, in her famous Southern accent, "what do ya'll do here?"

I didn't really understand the question. I'd just spent almost half an hour explaining Harvest Rain to her. Did she want me to explain again?

"Well, we create opportunities for emerging artists to pursue their passion in the theatre," I said, trying to put it in a nutshell.

"Yes, but what do you do?" she said again. "Do you know what you do?"

I was stumped.

"Well, yes, we put on shows and…."

"You do God's work, that's the answer, Tim," she said, matter-of-factly. "God's work on earth. That's what you do."

Fair enough, I thought. If Kristin Chenoweth says so.

"I bet you get a lot of people trying to bring you down, don't you?" she said, knowingly.

"How did you know?"

"Because it's what happens when you're good at what you do," she said wisely. "You just remember, not everybody is going to like you or what you have to offer – don't worry about that. Don't try to impress others. Just try to impress yourself."

That's my lasting memory of that day. Kristin did a great interview, followed by a stunning masterclass, and we all had the most wonderful afternoon learning from this Broadway legend, but what I will always remember most about that day is the sage advice Kristin offered me – a precious pearl of wisdom – that I have carried with me ever since. Her words caused me to realise that I was putting an awful lot of energy into appeasing others, trying to get them to like me, trying to get them to approve of the company, trying to get them to stop throwing stones and saying nasty things. But I realised, it's just like Taylor Swift says – haters gonna hate! Any time you stand up tall, there's always going to be someone ready to tear you down, like the crab in the bucket trying to make a break for it being pulled back down by the other crustaceans. I had to tune the noise of negativity out. I had to zone it out completely, and just focus on getting where I was going, doing what I wanted to do, stay committed to putting some good into the world and ignore what naysayers had to say. I'd been trying to impress the haters as a way of getting them to like me when what I should have done was just try to impress myself.

I arrived home late that night and ran myself a shower, and as I stood under the water, I got lost in thought, mulling over the events of the day and the advice Kristin had given me.

Impress myself, I thought over and over again.

Impress myself.

What would impress me?

What could I do to impress myself?

I hadn't asked myself that question in a long time.

Back at the beginning, when I was just dreaming, long before I set out and started achieving, I dreamed without fences, and I dreamed without expectation, and I dreamed without worrying what other people would think or say. Somewhere along the way, I had started conforming my dream to what I thought others wanted, to make them happy, to make them like me. No more. Now I wanted to impress myself again.

So, what would really impress me?

Something big, I thought.

Something that had never been done before.

What if we produced a show that had a fully professional principal cast surrounded by a large ensemble made up of our youth theatre and full-time students? Then we could involve everyone – the professionals would receive employment, and the up and coming young artists would receive opportunity.

That would impress me.

But how would we fit them on a regular stage? That would be a lot of people, I thought, and it would need a lot of space.

Perhaps we could do something in an arena.

In a big Entertainment Centre.

Yes, that would impress me.

Maybe we could do a musical in the arena.

Like a rock concert and a musical, all rolled into one.

Perhaps it could be a famous musical that everybody loves.

*Cats!*

Yes, *Cats!*

Everybody loves *Cats.*

Imagine: hundreds of performers dressed as cats.

That would impress me!

And Marina Prior could play Grizabella.

Yes, yes, I'd be so impressed!

I may have caused a drought from the longest shower in history that night, but I didn't care. I was waterlogged but buzzing with a new dream. I felt like the crab who'd made it out of the bucket. I didn't feel bound by what everyone else was thinking any more. I wasn't trying to please them.

I was just trying to please me.

At work the next day, I gathered the six full-time staff members who worked at Harvest Rain together in my office and outlined all of the ideas I had dreamed up in the shower the night before.

"I want to put on an arena production of *Cats* with hundreds of performers and starring Marina Prior."

I kid you not, that's exactly how I said it, and you can imagine their reaction. They all thought I'd gone round the twist. Maybe I had, but I felt so energised at the idea of doing something that *I* wanted to do, not something I thought everyone else wanted me to do. It felt real and authentic and exciting, and I was determined to see it happen.

Our General Manager, Megan Whiting, came up to me after the staff meeting and said:

"Are we really going to do all of this?"

"I want to," I said, "I really want to."

"But have you considered the cost?" she inquired. "Is any of it viable?"

"Well, look, let's just see if we can get Andrew Lloyd Webber to give us the rights first. Then we'll have to get the Entertainment Centre to give us the dates we want in the school holidays. And then I'll have to get Marina to say yes. We won't go ahead unless we get all three of those things to happen."

Megan seemed appeased by my response. She knew there was a pretty slim chance that all three of those things would happen, so I think she resolved to argue about the details later if the whole thing ever actually came to pass. Meanwhile, I was gently challenging the universe to deliver if I was supposed to move forward or to pull the rug out from under me if I wasn't.

As it turned out, the universe was right on my side.

When I spoke to Andrew Lloyd Webber's people, they gave us the rights to *Cats* without hesitation. Then I spoke to the folk at the Entertainment Centre, and it turned out they had a totally free week in the July school holidays and booked us in immediately. And when I called Marina to ask her to play Grizabella, she replied with a resounding "yes".

Well, you could have knocked Megan Whiting down with a feather.

Truth be told, I don't think I even thought we had half a chance of achieving a quarter of the things I dreamed up in the shower that night. It just goes to show that when you stop trying to impress everyone else and start trying to just impress yourself, you can line yourself up with the magic of the universe. You align with your own truth - that which is inherent in you – and the universe rises up to meet you.

Whenever you step out boldly, whenever you stand up tall, whenever you reach for the stars, you can be sure there will be somebody - or many somebodies - ready and waiting to take you down.

Your ambition shines a light on their shortcomings.

Their jealousy cannot handle your determination.

They become crabs in that bucket, trying to break your legs and keep you small. But when those crabs come crawling up to you, there's just one thing you have to remember.

YOU. ARE. NOT. A. CRAB.

You can get out of the bucket!

They may want to nip at you with their claws, and tug at you and snap at you with all their might, but while they are being their best crabby self, don't you ever forget that YOU ARE NOT A CRAB!

Those crabs have got nothing on you.

Those crabs can't take you down.

You're big. They're small.

Their claws are no match for you.

No bucket can hold you.

So never mind the crabs.

You climb on out of that bucket and pay them no attention.

You launch yourself up and out.

Impress yourself.

Outdo yourself.

Never mind those crabs.

They're not worth your time.

They're not worth your energy.

Stand on their heads and climb on out of that bucket.

Go dream your biggest dreams, and make them all come true.

## CHAPTER NINE
# THE BEST LIES BEYOND THE FEAR

Have you met my friend named Fear?

He comes to visit me every now and then.

He turns up every time I try to do something bigger than myself. Each time I step out and attempt to do something a little beyond what I'm used to, Fear comes to visit and reminds me that I best not do whatever it is that I'm trying to do, and that I should head back home where it's safe and nothing can harm me, and nothing can go wrong.

Fear is very concerned for my safety, it seems.

It's all Fear ever talks about.

*"Don't do this, you might get hurt."*

*"Don't do that, you might regret it."*

*"Don't go there, you mightn't like it."*

*"Don't try that, you might fail."*

Fear is unusually obsessed with keeping me safe.

Fear wants to keep me out of harm's way.

Fear doesn't want anything bad to happen to me.

In fact, Fear would like it if nothing at all ever happened to me; if I just stayed home, doors locked, windows closed, smothered in bubble wrap and hidden under the covers where nothing could get me or hurt me or harm me, then Fear would be very happy indeed.

But I don't think I would be.

In 2014, when we set about producing the largest production of *Cats* ever staged in the world, I got very used to little visits from my friend Fear. Most days, the experience of producing that show was simultaneously exhilarating while also being absolutely terrifying. I didn't know the first thing about putting on an arena production – I was just guessing my way to opening night. Thankfully, my best friend Callum had some experience choreographing school spectaculars featuring hundreds of young performers, so I bestowed upon him the task of directing and choreographing the production and masterminding exactly how we were going to stage a show with so many hundreds of performers all dressed as felines. In our initial planning for the show, we anticipated that we would have thirty professional performers on stage surrounded by an ensemble of maybe two hundred students from our youth theatre and full-time course, but that quickly snowballed out of control when over 800 children applied to be part of the mass ensemble. Callum was crafty enough to be able to find a place in the show for each of them – the stage was just large enough to hold them all! Managing a cast the size of a small village became like a military operation, with basic things like communications proving enormously complicated due to the volume of emails we had to send, not to mention the challenge of sourcing costumes and accessories for each of them to wear on stage.

800 leotards.

800 wigs.

800 make-up kits.

1600 parents with lots and lots (and lots) of questions.

Mounting that production stretched the Harvest Rain team to the absolute limits, and it stretched our finances as well. Back in the Sydney Street Theatre days, we had been able to produce a whole musical for as little as $50,000, sometimes even $25,000 if we were savvy. Once we moved to QPAC, costs escalated, and productions started costing between $300,000 to $500,000. When we crunched the numbers on *Cats*, we knew we would need to sell $1million in ticket sales just to cover the costs of mounting the production.

One million dollars!

ONE. MILLION. DOLLARS!

Every time I thought about that number, my stomach took a nose-dive like an elevator plummeting from a penthouse. We didn't have one million dollars! We were still operating from show to show, just trying to scrape by. Our hope was that by closing night we would have sold enough in ticket sales to be able to pay all the bills we had racked up in the hiring of the venue, the lights, the sound, the set, the costumes, the actors, the musicians and all the other costs associated with the show. It's the way we had always done it, but gambling $50,000 on a show at Sydney Street wasn't quite the same as gambling $1million on a big arena show in an Entertainment Centre.

The whole thing was a huge gamble.

Absolutely huge.

Everything was on the line, and if it didn't work, we were done and dusted.

It would be the end of Harvest Rain, for real this time, I realised.

So, most days I would come to work, and the staff would ask me how I was going, and I would respond by saying "I'm fine, just swimming in a pool of fear." And that's how it really felt – like I was up to my neck in it, and everywhere I looked were things that terrified me. The fear was relentless.

It was with me at work.

It was with me at home.

It was with me when I went to bed.

It was there waiting for me when I woke up.

Everywhere I went, there too was my friend Fear.

It was totally debilitating, constantly feeling anxious and

overwhelmed. "Why am I doing this?" I wondered out loud one day, as I lay in the fetal position on the couch in my office. What was my reason for pushing on, against all common sense and despite Fear constantly screaming at me to turn back? I wasn't sure. My mind felt busy and cluttered, so I closed my eyes, and in the darkness of my mind, I tried to search for peace.

Breathe in.

Breathe out.

Breathe in.

Breathe out.

Fear seems to diminish when I regulate my breathing. I don't know the science behind it, but it's a thing. In the same way Doubt had vanished when I got still and quiet, I found that when I focused on my breathing, I began to see the way forward with clarity, and Fear would subside. And so, as I lay there, slowly breathing in and out, I saw in my mind the faces of all the hundreds of children and teenagers who were rehearsing each weekend to be part of the show. They seemed to be so full of happiness, so determined, so energised; they reminded me of myself when I was a kid, dreaming of a life in the theatre. I could almost hear their voices beckoning me on, calling me forwards, cheering me onwards. There was something they needed from me, it seemed; something they needed me to do.

I wanted to help them.

I wanted to give them what they needed.

I wanted to muster up the courage to forge ahead on their behalf and in their honour, to battle beyond my Fear and create a place for them, pave the way for them, and blaze a trail for them to follow.

They were my reason for moving forward.

They were my reason to be brave.

So, on their behalf, I began facing Fear head on and addressing it by name.

Each morning when I woke up, and my friend Fear was still there, I would say out loud to it, "Thank-you for being here and for pointing out the imminent danger. I am well aware of it, and your services are not required at this time."

And as the day wore on and fear would rise again, I would say "Thank-you, but I don't have time to address your concerns right now, I'll get back to you later."

And then, as my head hit the pillow each night and thoughts of panic swirled through my head, I would say to my friend Fear, "Thank-you, but it's time for me to rest now. I'll deal with you another time."

And then I would do it all over again the next day.

It became a bit of a ritual for me, speaking to Fear and kind of making friends with it, thanking it for showing up in an effort to keep me safe, but letting it know I didn't need a bodyguard right this minute, and then walking right on through it. Fear can be a bully, but like most bullies, it caves when confronted.

So I forged on, fighting tooth and nail every day to keep the engines running and the wheels turning, until - contrary to Fear's predictions - our arena production of *Cats* did indeed go on to sell over $1million in ticket sales, fully recouping its costs and becoming the highest selling production in the history of Harvest Rain and the largest theatrical production of *Cats* ever staged in the world.

By pushing through the Fear, we had created something entirely unique in the world – a theatrical experience that allowed hundreds of young performers to live their dream, celebrate their passion and to feel validated doing what they love with people who were just like them. It didn't really dawn on us until we were actually watching the show that nothing like this had ever been seen before anywhere in the world – it was really, extremely unusual to see a traditional musical being staged in a non-traditional arena space with a cast of over 800 performers. Nobody does that (and possibly for good reason, because it's really bloody hard!). We had inadvertently created a whole new style of theatre that gave hundreds of young performers the chance to connect with and perform alongside seasoned professionals who were doing what those young performers all one day hoped to do. It was the dreamers meeting the doers, and the experience was transformational for so many of our young performers (and for many of our principals as well). After the closing night, my email inbox was flooded with messages from parents whose children had been in the mass ensemble saying how much the experience had meant to their child. For some, it was their first experience on stage, and it had ignited an enormous passion for performing and creative expression. For others, it was the first time they had ever found friends because it was their first time around so many like-minded people. We received emails from kids who said that they had never felt loved or accepted before being part of the arena experience with Harvest Rain. Some of the emails were heartbreaking, filled with stories of kids who had attempted suicide or self-harm due to loneliness and lack of self-worth, but through Harvest Rain's arena show they had found friends who loved them and people who accepted them, and it had given them something to really live for.

We were all pretty gobsmacked.

We had thought at the beginning we were just producing a show, but it turned out to be so much more than that for so many hundreds of young people. As I read those emails, I felt enormously grateful that I had been able to find the internal fortitude to push through the overwhelming Fear that stood between me and making the arena show happen. If I ever needed proof that the best really does lie beyond the Fear, then I needn't have looked further than that first arena show.

Of course, I did end up looking further.

After seeing the incredibly positive effect that the arena show had on the young members of our mass ensemble, I knew we had to do more. The children (and the parents) who had been in the mass ensemble were banging the door down for another performance opportunity, so we started pondering what other shows might work in the arena format. Having produced *Hairspray* a few years earlier, I knew it would transfer well into the arena, with plenty of scope for the mass ensemble to take the stage as kids from Baltimore, so we secured the rights and began making plans to stage *Hairspray – The Big Fat Arena Spectacular* as Harvest Rain's second major arena production. But this time, I wanted to involve more young performers than we had in *Cats*. I wanted to go bigger, extend our reach and let more young people take part in the life-changing arena experience.

"There are talented kids in every city, you know," I said to the staff one day in the Harvest Rain office. "This show could really work in any capital city. We should tour it."

"How in the world would you tour a show this big to another city?" Megan said, choking on her morning coffee at the thought of following me down the rabbit hole on yet another Tim O'Connor gamble. "We'd be putting at least 70 people on a plane, and accommodating them, and trucking the huge set and all the sound and lights – it would cost us a fortune."

And she was right. It certainly would cost a fortune – somewhere in the vicinity of $5million for a four-city tour I estimated. But the faces of all those children were in my mind again, and this time they were joined by more faces from all over the country, gently calling me onwards. It was as if they really needed something from me – from us – and if we could just be brave enough, we could provide them with an experience that could really change their lives.

It felt right.

As scary as it looked, I wanted to walk that path.

Surely, I thought, if we could make the show work in Brisbane, we could make it work in other places too?

I sent out a few emails to Entertainment Centres across Australia, just to see if any of them had availability on the rough dates I was thinking of. As it turned out, Newcastle had an opening in the July holidays, Adelaide could take us in October and Perth had a slot free in early January the following year. Each of them was eager to help us make the show work in their venue, so we made pencil bookings and started planning our very first arena tour – in fact, our very first tour, period!

At the start of the journey, it felt like business as usual, retracing the steps we had walked on *Cats*. Another 800 young performers signed up to be part of the show in Brisbane and before rehearsals began, we put them all through a weekend training boot-camp that prepared them for the rigours of the rehearsal room. Many of our young performers had never set foot on stage before, and we wanted to give them a meaningful training experience and not just simply push them out on stage, so participants paid a fee to take part in this boot camp and received a certificate once they had completed the weekend course, and then rehearsals began in earnest. Each weekend, our mass ensemble would gather for rehearsals in a huge basketball stadium alongside the incredible all-star cast of Australian entertainment industry icons we had pulled together. *Home & Away* star Tim Campbell played Corny Collins, theatre veterans Amanda Muggleton, Wayne Scott Kermond and Simon Burke played the roles of Velma, Wilbur & Edna respectively and Aria award winner Christine Anu played Motormouth Maybelle, all led by the incredible Lauren McKenna in the lead role of Tracy Turnblad. Callum was at the helm once again as Director and Choreographer, weaving his magic with so many hundreds of people on stage. After many weeks of refining and finessing the show, *Hairspray – The Big Fat Arena Spectacular* opened in Brisbane in April 2016, and it proved so popular with audiences that it eclipsed even the stratospheric success of our arena production of *Cats*. The mass ensemble lifted the roof each performance, particularly when they all stormed the staged for the high-octane, relentlessly energetic finale number *"You Can't Stop the Beat"*. The show was infectiously joyous.

Audiences lapped it up and the Brisbane season completely sold out, giving us all an incredible confidence boost as we prepared to send the show off on our first ever tour.

The show arrived in Newcastle in July 2016, where 500 young performers from the local area who had completed their boot camp were eagerly awaiting their opportunity to be rehearsed into the production. It was our first experience of having to re-teach the choreography to a whole new horde of children and then stitch the show back together, connecting the mass show up with the principal show in the week prior to performances. The young members of the Newcastle mass ensemble were highly enthusiastic, and it was great to see so many young people relishing the opportunity to connect with like-minded people and find their place as part of our creative community. Unfortunately, audiences in Newcastle seemed less enthusiastic – being our first time in town, they'd never really heard of Harvest Rain or the arena show before and selling tickets proved incredibly challenging. The tour was turning out to be enormously expensive – well over a million dollars was on the line just for the Newcastle season. While we were delighted with the opportunity to have a meaningful impact on the lives of so many young people, it was hard to watch the daily sales reports come in and not completely freak out at the thought of potentially losing a small fortune on our first venture outside of Brisbane. Two weeks before opening night in Newcastle, we were still more than $300,000 away from meeting our financial break-even for that leg of the tour, and the Fear really started to set in.

*"What will happen if we don't break even?"* I wondered.

*"How will we pay our bills?"*

*"How will we have enough money to get the show to the next city on the tour."*

It felt like my friend Fear was just screaming at me all day long.

From the minute I woke up to the moment I went to bed, Fear was running around with his pants on fire screaming, *"Fire in the hull! Fire in the hull! Abort! Abort! Mayday! Mayday! We're going down!"*.

The more I thought about the potential risk and the possible looming disaster that lay ahead, the more afraid I became. I was no longer swimming in a pool of fear – it was now an ocean, and the waves were overwhelming me.

A week before opening night as I lay in bed in my hotel room in Newcastle, I remembered a Bible story I had been told as a kid in Sunday school about when Jesus' disciples went out in a boat and a great storm rose up around them, and they were terrified by the waves. They cried out to Jesus to save them but found that he was actually out in the midst of the storm, out on the waves, walking on the water. Peter, one of the disciples, called out to Jesus, and Jesus beckoned him to walk out to meet him. Peter was terrified looking at the waves and knew that it was impossible to walk on water even in the best of conditions, but nonetheless, there was Jesus out amid the swell, just standing on top of the water. So, Peter stepped out of the boat and to his disbelief, as his foot touched the water, he did not sink but could walk like Jesus atop the waves. He took a few steps and then looked down at the crashing waves all around him, and the fear set in, and he began to sink. Jesus told him to look up, to ignore the waves around him and keep his eyes forward, looking towards where he was going, and only then would he not drown. And so, Peter looked away from the waves and began once again walking on water.

It occurred to me that the daily sales reports were like those waves crashing all around Peter – looking at them made me feel afraid, and I needed to look up and look where I was going if I wanted to avoid drowning under the weight of the Fear. I decided to make a conscious effort to stop looking at the daily sales reports – at this point, with a week to go, it would be what it would be. I wasn't going to panic about it anymore. I wasn't going to be afraid. I was going to look up, look ahead, look where I was going, and stop aligning myself with the energy of my Fear. Standing in the rehearsal room each day with the hundreds of young performers as they prepared to take part in the show, I decided to feed off their energy and their positivity instead. I decided to keep my focus on that, on the benefit it was having on their lives and on the impact the experience was having on their families.

Each day, we would hear stories of children who had always been an outcast at school and had never had friends until they came to be part of this show and for the first time in their life encountered like-minded people who loved and accepted them. There was one little girl who had endured numerous operations in her short twelve years on earth to deal with multiple tumours on her brain, and as a result she suffered significant anxiety and seizures which had stalled her mental development; she was twelve years old, but mentally she had not progressed beyond an eight-year-old, and as a result, he peers at school often ridiculed her or simply ignored her completely. Her mother told us how heartbreaking it was to drop her daughter at school each day and watch all the other children ignore her when she greeted them, but that since starting rehearsals, she had made so many wonderful friends who treated her "like a rock star", greeting her enthusiastically each day, that she hadn't experienced a single seizure or anxiety attack in the whole rehearsal period.

The experience had completely changed this little girl's life.

That's what I wanted to focus on.

As big as my Fear seemed to be at times, what we were doing was way bigger. We were creating a safe haven for creative young people, a safe place for young dreamers; this was important and meaningful, and I chose to give my focus to that, and never mind the sales reports.

Change the energy, I thought, change the focus, change the outcome.

And it worked.

Almost as if by a miracle, there was a sudden rush of ticket sales in the final days before the show opened in Newcastle, and by closing night the show had just managed to cover its costs. We scraped through by the skin of our teeth, and I began to learn the value of focus and started paying attention to what I gave my attention to.

If I aligned with the energy of Fear, I spiralled downwards into more fearful feelings, and attracted outcomes that resonated with the Fear.

If I raised my eyes and looked forward, gave my focus to the incredible energy of the children in the mass ensemble, focused on the good we were putting into the world, the things that seemed to be going wrong around me found a way of taking care of themselves. The waves lapping at my feet did not require my attention.

Eyes forward. Onwards!

As we moved the show on to Adelaide, we gathered another 700 children to take part in the mass ensemble and set about teaching them the dance steps and integrating them into the show. The cost of flying the cast and crew and moving the set, lights and sound across the country really put a strain on the budget, and even though audiences turned out in droves to see the show, the tour to Adelaide ended up costing so much money that it became almost impossible for us to cover our costs. I tried hard not to look down – not to allow my Fear to overwhelm me – but losing money in Adelaide made moving forward exceedingly difficult and put added pressure on the final leg of the tour in Perth. We had to have a win there, I thought, or our goose was really cooked.

Thankfully, there was huge enthusiasm from young people in Perth who wanted to be in the show, and we ended up with just over 600 young performers signing up to be part of the mass ensemble. We took them all through their boot camp training and got them all buzzed about the showing coming to Perth in January 2017, but our plans hit a snag the minute we put the tickets for the show on sale. We had expected to see the usual rush for seats in the pre-sale that we had enjoyed on all of our arena shows to date, but on the first day of sales, we hardly sold a single ticket.

The second day of sales wasn't much better.

Two weeks in and we realised there was a big problem.

People in Perth just weren't buying tickets.

Maybe they didn't like the show?

Maybe they didn't know the venue?

Maybe there was too much going on in Perth for us to cut through?

Whatever the reason, the tickets weren't selling, and even when we ran television ads and implemented an extensive marketing campaign, nothing seemed to move those tickets. Two months out from opening night in Perth, we were faced with a difficult decision – proceed and run the risk of being at least half a million dollars short of what we needed to cover costs, or pump the brakes, cancel the show and refund the tickets that had been sold. At the end of the day, we were left with no choice – given the poor ticket sales, it just wasn't viable to proceed with the season in Perth.

We would have to cancel.

Well, my friend Fear had an absolute field day with this one.

*"What will the children say when they find out the show is cancelled?"*

*"What will their parents say?"*

*"What will the ticket buyers say?"*

*"What will the media say?"*

*"Will our reputation be ruined forever?"*

*"Have I just driven our company over a metaphorical cliff?"*

Swimming in the ocean of Fear once again.

I could feel myself being enveloped by the waves, completely consumed by Fear, afraid of what was going on and what would happen next. I tried with all my might to lift my eyes and look ahead, and in those moments of clarity, I knew that the most important thing to do was honour the children and the parents who had already committed to being part of the production, who had believed in us and put themselves through boot camp. It may not have been financially viable to bring the full multi-million dollar production of *Hairspray* to them, but we could still bring us. We could still turn up, we could still bring the stars of the show, we could still give them a week in January that they would never forget, a chance to connect with one another and to feel loved and validated.

We simply had to show up.

So we instructed the ticketing company to refund all those who had bought tickets, and we sent an email breaking the news of the cancellation to all the participants who had signed up to be part of the mass ensemble, letting them know that we would still be coming in January, with all of the stars, to put together a workshop and showcase for all of them to be part of in January instead. As far as consolation prizes, it was the best we could do in a difficult situation, and I felt confident that everyone would be understanding and supportive.

I could not have been more wrong.

The backlash was swift and overwhelming.

The hate mail we got during that time was really intense. While most of the participants took the disappointing news in their stride and said they would gladly join us in January for the consolation workshop and showcase, there was a section of the community in Perth who really went to town on us. They bombarded our social media with negative comments and flooded our inbox with hate mail, and our phones rang off the hook to the extent that we just had to stop answering them. One person was so incensed that they called a local current affairs program and they ended up running a story on us, accusing us of being "a scam" who had "ruined Christmas" for hundreds of children in Western Australia.

It was an absolute nightmare.

We understood that the decision to cancel had disappointed lots of people, but we also knew that there was nothing we could do about it. We couldn't hold guns to people's heads and make them buy tickets to see the show. It felt like we were under attack. I wanted to climb into my bed and dive under the covers and never come out again as long as I lived. I felt afraid to check my emails, and afraid to answer my phone, for fear that all I would find was more hate and more nastiness and more bad news and bad energy.

The fear started messing with my mind and planting irrational thoughts in my head. I began to envisage swarms of people waiting for us at the Perth airport in a picket line when we touched down for the consolation workshop in January. I pictured them throwing rotten vegetables at us as we attempted to collect our bags from the luggage carousel. I thought there would be people lined up at the venue with placards ready to spit on us on the first day of the workshop.

But Fear is a hypochondriac and an exaggerator.

In reality, when we got to Perth, there was no picket line or rotten vegetables. It turned out that the many hundreds of participants who had agreed they would still turn up to our consolation workshop were absolutely delightful, and all those who felt we had "ruined Christmas" went strangely silent, and we never heard from them the whole time we were there. We ended up having the most enriching experience in Perth working with those enthusiastic young people who were determined to stand by us and stand with us no matter what. At the end of the week, over two thousand people turned up to watch the final showcase and show their support for both the participants and for us, and I quietly shed a few tears of joy and sheer relief. My Fear had told me we would be annihilated in Perth, but in reality, we were embraced.

Turns out that Fear is a dirty, dirty liar.

At the end of the tumultuous *Hairspray* tour, I returned to Brisbane and as we set to work mounting a new arena production - this time of the perennial favourite, *Grease* - I realised that I was now living on the other side of Fear. All that swimming in the pool of Fear, and then drowning in the ocean of Fear, and then pushing forward no matter how much water swirled around me and no matter how many times I got dunked or bombarded by the swell, had led me to this place beyond Fear.

I felt brave now.

I felt resilient.

I felt confident that I knew how to weather the storm.

I knew Fear would rise again, but I felt sure that I knew what to do when it did.

I knew how to speak to it.

I knew how to calm it.

I knew how to soothe it.

I knew how to walk past it.

*Grease – The Arena Experience* opened in Brisbane in 2017 to another sold out season, before moving on to play in every other major capital city in Australia – a full seven-city tour. The lessons we had learned in walking through the Fear as we attempted to tour *Hairspray* around the country set us up well for the *Grease* tour, and we managed to cover costs in every city, performing to almost 100,000 people and involving over 5,000 young Australians in the production as we went.

As the final stop on the national tour, *Grease* was set to play in Perth. Even though everybody I spoke to said we should avoid ever going back to Perth because "shows just don't sell over there", I was determined to return as a sign of thanks to the kind souls who had stood by us in our hour of need. Everyone was afraid that returning to Perth at the end of the tour would mean another financial loss, but I refused to be a prisoner to Fear. We persisted, and we did our research, and we found a more central venue to perform in, and we invested in better marketing, and when *Grease* came to Perth at the end of the national tour, the people of Western Australia embraced the show so warmly that the sales there were the highest of any city we had visited previously, with over 15,000 people turning out to see the show over the weekend that it played at Perth Arena.

None of that could have happened had I not walked past my Fear.

Fear isn't as smart as it lets on.

It doesn't know so much.

It's a master at bluffing.

Fear will con you into thinking all kinds of crazy things. It will twist your mind up in knots and have you convinced that the sky is falling, if you let it.

You have to know that Fear and Truth are not the same things.

Fear deals only in fantasy, in what could be, and what might be, or what might not be or could never be.

What makes you think that Fear has all the answers?

What makes you think that Fear knows more than you do?

What makes you think that Fear is right?

What makes you think that Fear is worth listening to?

If your life is a table with many chairs, make sure you only give one seat to Fear. Fear can be a singular voice at the table, but you want to also leave seats for your Courage, and your Curiosity, your Determination, your Hope, your Compassion and, most importantly, your Joy.

Don't let Fear take over the table.

Sit him in the corner and let him know his place. He doesn't get to dominate every conversation. He doesn't get to sway every decision. You should listen to what Fear has to say, but then allow your Joy and your Courage to respond with kindness, saying:

*"Thank you for trying to keep me safe, but safe is not where I want to live.*

*I want to walk where there is no path.*

*I want to travel where there is no road.*

*I want to journey where there is no trail.*

*I want to find my way forward to new and exciting places.*

*I will transcend Fear.*

*Because I know as sure as the sun will rise that the best lies beyond the Fear.*

*And I will not be afraid."*

## CHAPTER TEN
# THE COLLECTIVE DREAM

There are dreams we dream that are entirely for ourselves.

I'd say most of our dreams are like that.

We want a new car.

We want more money in the bank.

Maybe a new house.

Better clothes.

A higher paying job.

In my opinion, spending time pondering how life could be better or more satisfying is a very good use of your time indeed. If the thought of how good things could be in the future makes you feel happier in your now, then I say that's the kind of dream you should be dreaming as often as is humanly possible.

But there's another kind of dream I've discovered that has some real magic attached to it. It feels different from the kind of "self-improvement" dreams listed above. It feels bigger somehow, or deeper, or heavier, but somehow lighter, and wider, and stranger, and more mysterious and ethereal, but at the same time, it feels very knowing and luminous and all-encompassing. It's hard to explain without sounding like a thesaurus, but basically, you know that you've stumbled upon real magic when the dream that you have bubbling inside of you touches on more than just what you can get for yourself.

It's bigger than just a nice new car for you to drive around in or a luxury beach holiday or an expensive pair of shoes or the latest tech gadget.

It's a dream that reaches out and touches other dreams in the minds of other people.

It connects and intersects with other people's needs and wants and desires.

It lays a foundation on which others can build.

It provides a platform on which others can launch their own dream.

It's not just about you.

It's about us.

It's about all of us.

It's what I've come to know as the "Collective Dream". To me, it's the place where the magic of the universe really does live and breathe and have its being.

We exist to contribute to the expansion of all things.

I really believe that.

That's why we're here.

Our purpose is to create, to expand, to add to what already is, and to make more. When we dream, we become architects of that expansion, and as our dreams become a reality the universe literally expands and grows and evolves on the wings of our imagination and the whims of our dreams. When we dream the Collective Dream, we dream in concert with those around us and those who have gone before us. We dream in connection with the past as a bridge to the future; we hold hands metaphorically with the Dreamers of old whose visions laid the foundation for our own dreaming and whose shoulders we now proudly stand on and build upon, and reach out to our fellow Dreamers who feel bound and inspired by the same things that light us up, and we dream as one piece of a much larger puzzle. You dream one piece, and I dream another, and so on and so on, until collectively the realisation of our dreams collide in a beautiful cacophony of imagination, all the pieces coming together just as the universe requires for perfect expansion and flawless evolution.

A magnificent jigsaw, a marvellous collection of dreams.

Through our dreams, our lives become stepping-stones for our own future dreaming, and for the dreaming of others. The realisation of one collective dream paves the way for the realisation of more, and more, and more, and so on, like a cosmic tapestry being woven together, one dream at a time.

There have been many times in my life when I have felt swept up in the Collective Dream. You can always tell when you're dreaming collectively because it always feels a little bigger than yourself. It always seems a little outside of your reach, and like you can't quite grasp what you have to do to realise the dream, but you know the dream is percolating all the same. It doesn't quite make sense, at least not yet anyway, but you know the clarity is coming, and if you just tune in – if you just lean in a little - the next little bit of the collective puzzle will become clear in time.

Sometimes it's like I'm listening to an old wireless radio that's struggling to find a signal. There's mostly crackling and hissing, but every now and then you hear the sound of a voice break through the static, and it gives clarity for a moment. As you turn the dials gently and gingerly strain to make out what is being transmitted, you slowly get a sense of the piece of the collective puzzle that has been bestowed upon you to bring forth.

Sometimes it takes days and weeks to make sense of.

Sometimes years.

Sometimes it's sparked by something someone says, and then someone else comes along and brings more clarity, and then another person, and after five different conversations, over five different days (or months....or years) your thinking culminates in the Collective Dream. You tap into something beyond yourself, beyond your own thinking. You dream the dream that is bigger than the one you dream for yourself.

Sometimes it will come to you at three in the morning when you wake up in bed and can't get back to sleep. (I always keep pen and paper on my bedside table for that very reason, because on occasion I have been woken up by inspiration and my pen couldn't scrawl across the page fast enough to write it all down.)

From time to time, I seem to be able to channel the Collective Dream when I'm in the shower or in the swimming pool. I've had some of my best ideas and moments of inspiration while submerged in a body of water. I can't explain it really, but I've been told that water can be a great conduit for divine inspiration, and thus a great place to channel your own Collective Dream.

Funnily enough, though, my most memorable encounter with a dream beyond that which I dream for myself didn't happen while I was swimming or bathing, or standing in a puddle or in a light shower of rain. In fact, there was no water in sight, and it wasn't three in the morning either. My most significant experience of channeling the Collective Dream actually had very little to do with the time of day or the wetness of my surrounds, and much more to do with the specifics of the company I was keeping that day.

You see it all started because the future King of England was running terribly late.

We'd been waiting for the Duke and Duchess of Cambridge to arrive for over an hour. I'm the kind of guy who likes things to run on time – I don't usually have much patience for lateness – but I guess when you're the heir to the British throne, I'm willing to bide my time.

Will and Kate were in Australia on their first royal tour as a couple, and I had been invited to the State Reception. It was a fairly small affair at a rooftop bar in the city with only about 150 guests in attendance, and we were all on a single invitation - no partners allowed - so everyone was standing by themselves, clutching a glass of champagne and trying hard to make small talk. I get really shy around people I don't know, so I was doing everything I could to stand to the side and make conversation with myself. As I guzzled as much free champagne as I could, I leaned out over the balcony to catch a glimpse of the crowds milling below, and a friendly looking guy with shaggy blonde hair sidled up to me and struck up a conversation.

"You know anyone here?" he said.

"No, not a soul", I replied.

"Me neither. You a red dot?" he said, looking down at my nametag.

"What's a red dot?" I asked.

"The dot on your tag," he said, pointing to the green dot on mine. "Red dots get to meet the Royals in person. Green dots get to stand at the back of the room and watch".

I breathed a sigh of relief.

"So, I don't have to meet them?".

"Nah, you're a green dot," he said. "You can just enjoy the free food and alcohol. The red dots are the ones who have to press the flesh".

Thank God, I thought.

A full A4 page of instructions had come with our invitation explaining exactly how we were expected to behave in the presence of royalty, and I'd been freaking out about forgetting the royal protocol and making an idiot of myself in front of the future King and Queen of England.

Only shake hands if they offer theirs.

Don't speak unless they speak to you first.

Bow or curtsey when they greet you.

Address them as "Your Royal Highness".

Only look at them if they look at you.

Do not feed them after midnight.

There were so many things to remember!

Shake hands.

Don't speak.

Do speak.

Bow, don't curtsey (you're not a lady).

Say "Your Highness", not "Your Majesty".

I was stressing out! What if I forgot and accidentally spoke before they did, or shook hands too vigorously, or forgot what to call them, or accidentally head-butted one of them? Would I be arrested? Exiled from the kingdom? Beheaded?

Thankfully, I wouldn't have to find out. Ah, bless you, lucky green dot, I thought to myself, as I sipped on my fourth glass of complimentary royal champagne. For the next half hour, I proceeded to stand in the corner of the room guzzling free wine and shovelling free food into my mouth like the famine was coming. I may have devoured an entire platter of cheese puffs. Don't judge me.

After what felt like an eternity, the royal motorcade pulled up on the street below, and we were corralled into position ready for the arrival of the royal couple; the red dots were brought to the front of the room, and a barricade was placed between them and the rest of us green dots at the back of the room, which was a good thing, because, by this time, most of us were well and truly drunk. It had been a long wait on a hot day with unlimited alcohol – can you blame us?

There was a sudden flurry of activity at the front of the room, a sea of flashbulbs and the click of many cameras, and then, at last, the Duke and the Duchess entered the room, led by the Premier of Queensland and his wife. The room was now basically made up of those who were red dotty enough to speak with the royals and the rest of us green dots that were standing around just watching them like creepers.

It was a weird situation, just watching them from the back of the room while trying hard not to topple over from the heat or the liquor.

It got instantly weirder when all of a sudden and most unexpectedly, Prince William breached the barricade of bollard and chain that segregated us lowly green dots from the red dots and started to casually walk among us, shaking hands with random green dots as he went. Kate followed, and soon a room full of highly inebriated people wearing name tags with green dots were being greeted by the future King of England.

"I have to get out of here now," I thought to myself.

I was too drunk to be meeting the milkman, let alone a member of the royal family.

I pushed through the crowds to head to the very back of the room and tried to disappear among a row of pot plants, but while I was doing that, the crowd in the room started to form a sort of semi-circle around the outskirts of the terrace, so the Duke and the Duchess had a clear path to walk the outside of the room and greet everyone individually. My plan to hide at the back of the room had now just put me at the centre of the giant semi-circle!

Then, to make matters worse, the Premier spotted me. He smiled and waved, and then he whispered to Prince William and gestured in my direction, and then lead him past the queue of guests eagerly awaiting their moment with royalty until he came to stand directly in front of me, with the Duchess not far behind.

"This is Tim O'Connor," said the Premier, introducing me. "He runs Harvest Rain Theatre Company".

Prince William reached out to shake my hand.

Do I take it?

I can't remember!

Am I allowed to touch him?

I'm freaking out!

My hand touched his, and I felt myself going into an involuntary curtsey but managed to stifle it and turn it into a bow before anyone noticed.

"Your Majesty," I stammered, immediately realising that was the exact thing I wasn't supposed to call him. Then I realised I was still shaking his hand, so I dropped it awkwardly and bowed again.

"Your Royal Highness," I stuttered, trying to not look like a complete alcoholic. "It's a pleasure to meet you." By this point, I wasn't even sure if I was still speaking English.

"This is my wife, Kate", William said, and Kate stepped forward and offered her hand, which I took and bowed again. Kate was easily the most beautiful creature I had ever laid eyes on up close. Her skin was flawless. Does she even have pores? I was quite close to her, and I have to say, I don't think she does. She was just bathed in perfection. Her hair was half up and half down, but the half that was up appeared to be held up by absolutely nothing as if her hair was so royal and magical that it had just weaved itself into whatever style she desired. She was breathtaking, in every sense of the word, and I was drunk. What a combination.

"Your Royal Highness," I blurted out, "Thank you for having me here today".

"Tell me about your theatre company", she said, looking genuinely interested.

"We produce musical theatre, and we create training and performance opportunities for young artists," I said, struggling to put words together into an intelligible sentence.

"That must keep you very busy" she inquired.

"Yes, it does," I said. "But it's very rewarding. I love helping young people follow their passion".

And then Kate gave me a knowing look like she was pondering something deeply meaningful.

Time sort of stopped for a second and everything went quiet.

I couldn't hear the noise of everyone else in the room anymore.

There was a kind of silence and a sense of expectation.

It wasn't just the alcohol. It was something else.

Something bigger than the moment we were in.

""Investing in young people is investing in the future," she said to me. "We are their stepping stones, the bridge to their dreams."

And that, right there, was the spark of the Collective Dream, conjured by the future heir to the throne, and passed on to little old me.

In that moment, where time seemingly stood still, I saw a vision in my mind of hundreds and thousands of young performers all gathered together, holding hands, right across the country, and across the world. I saw their faces, smiling, beaming, unified across the globe, joined by their love of the arts and of each other. They were like a network, all interconnected, and intertwined, all helping each other, and leaning on each other, and supporting one another.

Something Kate knew to be true sparked up against something I deeply understood, and for a moment there was this kind of synergy, this strange connectedness, this deep understanding, this common vision, and it lingered with me long after the moment had passed.

I don't remember what happened after that.

Did I talk more?

Did I thank her?

Did I say goodbye?

How did I get home?

I honestly don't remember.

But that moment with the Duchess and her words are burnt into my memory forever.

That brief conversation with her ignited something in me that burnt like a fire for the days and weeks that followed.

*A bridge to their dreams.*

I couldn't get that phrase out of my head.

*We are their stepping stones.*

Yes, that's right.

We are.

We lay down all that we are and all that we know so that those who follow us can stand on our shoulders and climb further and higher and go up and beyond. Those specific words sparked the image in my mind of the thousands of faces of young artists across the globe, all looking out towards me as if they were calling me. Yearning for something. Thousands of young hearts beckoning. I thought of our arena shows, and of the effect the whole experience was having on thousands of young creative people from all walks of life, and Kate's words played in my mind.

*We are a bridge to their dreams.*

*We are their stepping stones.*

I began to realise that what we were doing was not just putting on a show. It was much more than that. We were creating a network. A network of creative young people. Making a safe space for them all; a place where they all could belong, where they could share their passion and inspiration, connect and learn and journey onwards together.

We were their stepping stone.

We were the bridge to their dreams.

Over the years, it was always the memory of Kate's words and the power of the Collective Dream that fueled my efforts to grow Harvest Rain into what it has become today - the world's largest youth arts organisation. We are now a community with over 25,000 active members; the largest gathering of creative young people on the planet. Our organisation has become a major hub for creative youth, a safe space for artistic teens where they can grow and learn and connect and be inspired, and the evolution of our company into this immense and powerful gathering was triggered by that chance drunken encounter with a Princess, when we both harnessed a single puzzle piece of the Collective Dream, and the magic of the universe began its work.

Those are the dreams I now yearn for; the dreams that go beyond what I can dream for myself and delve into what can be dreamed for the benefit and betterment of others. They satisfy me more deeply than my personal dreams. They feel like a contribution, or like an offering. They are the kind of dreams that feel electric in the dreaming, and then in the realisation, I can almost feel the universe literally expanding as it grows to make space for this glorious new creation born from the Collective Dream.

As you go about the business of dreaming big and living brave, my hope for you is that you will experience the joy of dreaming beyond yourself and out into the collective. I hope that you will know the astonishing joy and satisfaction that comes from birthing a dream that is bigger than yourself and realizing a dream that contributes to the expansion of all things. I pray that you will come to know that it truly is the meaning of life – to dream so fiercely and so courageously and so outrageously that the universe literally expands and grows and evolves to make room for the realization of what was once just in your mind, but now lives and breathes and takes up space in the world.

There is magic in this world, ready and waiting to delight and inspire you, to harness what is created in your imagination and usher it out into the world. You are a dreamer, and you are a doer, and what lives in your mind can also live in your reality, if you have the courage and the determination to relentlessly pursue it.

Be brave, my friend.

Be bold.

Dream big.

And go make all your dreams come true.

I dare you!

DREAM
BIG
LIVE
BRAVE

♡TIM
xx

# ACKNOWLEDGEMENTS

I started writing this book in 2015 on a long plane trip from Brisbane to Perth (five hours in the air, and when you land you're still in the same country – welcome to Australia!). I was bored and couldn't find anything to watch on the in-flight entertainment, so I started to write on my laptop. Five hours and eight thousand words later, I had tapped out the beginnings of this book. As we disembarked, I mentioned to Megan Whiting that I'd accidentally started writing a book, and she was so enthusiastic about it that it spurred me to continue writing. Every plane trip I took in the weeks, months and years that followed became a great opportunity to write, and slowly the book began to take shape. I didn't realise at the time that it would take me years to complete; there were still lessons for me to learn, and I was still living the end of the book. Indeed, I think in many ways that I'm still living the book as I write this, still learning, still crafting new life chapters. Perhaps there will be more books to write in the years to come, once I've recovered from the writing of this one!

After almost four years of writing and re-writing in airports and airplanes all over the world, I had started to give up hope that I might ever actually finish this book. I wondered if it might always just be this incomplete thing that my children would one day dig out of a drawer long after I'd died and ponder what my half-finished musings meant. It wasn't until the end of 2018 that an unexpected email from a sixteen-year-old girl from South Australia triggered an urgency in me to put pen to paper and finish what I'd started. Billie-Rose had been in our arena production of *Hairspray* in Adelaide, and had been so inspired by what we were doing that she put herself on a plane and came to do work experience at Harvest Rain with us during production week for the premiere season of *Grease – The Arena Experience* in Brisbane in 2017. I was thoroughly impressed with her tenacity and drive, and in conversation with her during that time I asked her what she wanted to do with her life.

"I want to run my own theatre company," she replied with a glint in her eye that was all too familiar to me. She reminded me of myself two decades earlier, and I told her so.

"Well, what's stopping you?" I said. "Get on with it."

She looked a bit shocked at my bluntness, so I reassured her.

"You don't have to wait until you're old to do the things you want to do," I explained. "Just get on with it now!"

She smiled politely, and then I was whisked away into the hustle and bustle of production week, and to be honest I forgot all about the conversation until Billie's email came through just before Christmas in 2018 letting me know that she'd successfully applied for a grant to start her own theatre company. She'd gathered a bunch of friends and at the age of sixteen was the Artistic Director of her own company, producing theatre for young people in Adelaide.

I was so proud of her. At such a young age, she was really kicking goals. When I asked her what made her think to apply for the grant, she said "Well, you told me to get on with it, so I did."

It shocked me that Billie had taken my passing comment as permission to follow her dreams, and I felt an enormous amount of responsibility to help guide her on what I knew would be an exciting, thrilling and all at once terrifying adventure.

So I opened my laptop and opened the book I had been writing for four years and committed myself to finishing it, for Billie-Rose and all the other young Dreamers out there like her who could use a mud map that detailed the perils and perks of following your dreams. I chained myself to the desk for weeks, determined to write down what I knew, what I had learned, the mistakes I had made and all the hard-fought wins, even if it killed me. Most days, it felt like giving birth. Excruciatingly exhausting, painful and agonizing, but at the same time exhilarating and joyous and satisfying.

I'm so glad it's done, I'm so glad it happened, I'm so glad it's over, and now here is this book, out in the world, flying freely. Dreams turning to reality. I love it.

So, in many ways, I have much to thank Billie-Rose for. As much as I inspired her, she also inspired me; if she hadn't sent that email, who knows if I would ever have finished this book, so thank-you very much, Billie-Rose. Keep dreaming BIG, my friend.

Thank-you to Megan Whiting, who always spurred me on in the writing of this book, and Steph Sanders and Grant Couchman, to you too. And Sally Townsend, who was one of the first people to read a draft of this thing – your encouragement meant the world to me. Thank-you.

To Callum Mansfield, who deserves more credit for his contribution to my life and its many lessons than this book could contain. When I met him twenty years ago, who knew that not only would a beautiful friendship blossom, but also an entirely new genre of arena entertainment. Thanks Cazzy for your constant loyalty and love, which is hidden behind every word in this book.

To my Mum, without whom there really wouldn't be anything to write about in this book. I love you Mum.

To my son, Henson, and my daughter, Phoenix, thank-you for amusing yourselves for most of that Christmas holidays while Daddy furiously typed away in the spare room finishing this thing off. I love you both to the moon and back.

To Robbie & David Parkin – your influence on my life has been more profound than words can conjure, and this book would be a pile of blank pages were it not for all that you gave me, in your time, your care, your guidance and your trust. I will always be grateful to you both, because I know that I am who I am because of who you were to me. You paved the way, and you have my eternal gratitude.

Thank-you to my Dennett, who says he hardly needs to read this book because he lives it with me every day. He's stood by my side not just through the writing of this book but through the living of a great deal of the scariest parts of it. You help me to be brave. Love you monkey, always.

To all the people mentioned in this book who were part of my journey and who helped me learn so many valuable lessons, good and bad, I thank you all. And to those of you who weren't mentioned but were with me along the way, my heart is full with gratitude for you as well.

To the whole team at Harvest Rain, you're the best people to come to work with every day. Thank you for daring with me on a daily basis.

To the thousands of young people who are part of our company from all walks of life and form all corners of the globe, this book really is for you. You bring us all such joy and it is my life's greatest honour to be able to speak into your lives and shine a light on your path. May you all do even bigger, better and greater things than me as you travel down life's path.

And to you reading this book – thanks for taking the time to pick it up and give it a look. It means a lot to me, it really does. Thank-you.

Love and light. Keep dreaming BIG! Onwards!

# ABOUT THE AUTHOR

Based in Brisbane, Australia, Tim O'Connor is the CEO of the world's largest not-for-profit youth arts organisation, Harvest Rain.

Tim grew up dreaming of a life in the theatre, and over the last twenty years has built an impressive career not only as a theatre director and producer, but also as a mentor, a teacher and an inspirational speaker. Through his work in the world of musical theatre, he has built a platform from which he encourages people from all walks of life to think big, live brave and dare to follow their dreams.

Tim has received 9 Del Arte Chart awards for his work in the theatre and won a Groundling Award for Outstanding Contribution to the Queensland Theatre Industry. He was nominated as Brisbane Person of the Year and won a gold Matilda Award for his work with Harvest Rain.

Tim is passionate about helping young creative people pursue their passion and follow their dreams. As such, he is the founder of both the Brisbane Academy of Musical Theatre (BAMT) and regularly teaches and mentors emerging young artists. He also hosts his own weekly podcast, *TimTime;* and regularly shares his inspirational views on life both on his podcast and on his social media pages.

A father of two, Tim is a relentless daredevil dreamer, committed to helping others to dream BIG and dare to make those dreams come true.

www.timoconnor.net.au